# JON BONNELL'S

★★★ FINE
# TEXAS
## CUISINE

# JON BONNELL'S

★★★ FINE
TEXAS
CUISINE

## JON BONNELL

### PHOTOGRAPHS BY B. J. LACASSE

GIBBS SMITH
TO ENRICH AND INSPIRE HUMANKIND

Salt Lake City | Charleston | Santa Fe | Santa Barbara

First Edition
13 12 11 10        7 6 5 4 3

Published by
Gibbs Smith
P.O. Box 667
Layton, Utah 84041

1-800.835.4993 orders
www.gibbs-smith.com

Designed and produced by mGraphicDesign
Printed and bound in China
Gibbs Smith books are printed on either recycled, 100% post-consumer waste, FSC-certified papers or on paper produced from a 100% certified sustainable forest/controlled wood source.

Library of Congress Cataloging-in-Publication Data
Bonnell, Jon.
  Fine Texas cuisine / Jon Bonnell ; photographs by B. J. Lacasse, unless otherwise noted. — 1st ed.
     p. cm.
  ISBN-13: 978-1-4236-0523-2
  ISBN-10: 1-4236-0523-3
 1. Cookery, American—Southwestern style. 2. Cookery—Texas. I. Title.
  TX715.2.S69B66 2009
  641.5979—dc22
                          2008054228

*To both of my parents who taught me how to cook from a very young age:*

*To my mother, D'Ann, an outstanding classic cook in her own right, for involving me in the kitchen even before I could read. I still remember picking out pictures from cookbooks and making special dinners with mom.*

*To my father, Bill, who taught me to cook from a "seat of your pants" approach and who taught me a love and respect for the outdoors.*

# ★ ★ ★
# CONTENTS

# ACKNOWLEDGMENTS

I'd like to give a very special thanks to all of the local farms and ranches that truly produce the finest ingredients anyone could ever ask for. For all of those who put in the backbreaking work and have dedicated their lives to growing and harvesting products with the highest standards of excellence and environmentally ethical standards, I thank each of you from the bottom of my heart. It is only with the finest ingredients that I can even begin to create Fine Texas Cuisine. The following Texas farms and ranches have all contributed to the success of Bonnell's in one way or another:

Brazos Valley Cheese, Waco: Handmade all-natural cheeses

Broken Arrow Ranch, Ingram: Hill Country venison and antelope

Burgundy Pasture Beef, Grandview: Organic, grass-fed angus beef

Deborah's Farmstead Goat Cheese, Fort Worth: Handmade all-natural cheeses

Diamond H Ranch, Bandera: Texas gourmet quail

Dominion Farms, Denison: Free-range organic chicken, eggs, and pork

Frontier Meats, Fort Worth: Texas wild boar, ostrich, buffalo, and all-natural beef

The Haute Goat Creamery, Lubbock: Handmade goat cheeses

Homestead Gristmill, Elm Mott: Stone ground grits

La Casa Verde, Weatherford: Organic hydroponic microgreens, specialty herbs, and tomatoes

Young's Greenhouse, Charlie: Organic baby lettuces

I'd like to thank chef Ed McOwen, a longtime friend, co-owner of Bonnell's Restaurant, and one of the finest chefs in the country, for his participation and help, not only in developing this book, but for his selfless approach in helping create what we call "Fine Texas Cuisine."

A special thanks to all of the dedicated staff at Bonnell's, who work tirelessly day after day to keep our business on top. For those I affectionately call "Lifers," who have been with me since day one: Thank you, Pedro, Reyna, Lilia, Maria, Ari, Pablo, and Sheila. Long live the opening team! Thank you, Andreas, for keeping the front of the house up to the standards of the food for the past three years and for your personal dedication to the service industry. Thanks to sous chefs Fletcher and Pedro for their long hours and commitment to nothing short of perfection every day, on every plate. I would also like to thank Jenevieve Croall, who keeps me organized and has worked just as hard as I have to make this book a reality.

And mostly I thank my wife, Melinda, for her understanding and patience as we ride this crazy rollercoaster of a life together. As they say, the only thing crazier than being a chef is being married to one. I can hardly wait until our daughter, Charlotte, is old enough to read this book! ★

# ★ ★ ★
# INTRODUCTION

## WHAT IS "FINE TEXAS CUISINE"?

When I opened my first restaurant, I named it Bonnell's, Fine Texas Cuisine as a way of defining my own personal culinary style. The concept was somewhat misunderstood at first since "fine dining" and Texas haven't always been synonymous. The confusion would go something like this:

"The sign here says you serve Texas food," a patron would remark.
"Yes, sir," I'd confidently reply.
"So is that Mexican, barbecue, or chicken-fried steaks?"
"Well, the sign does say TEXAS, but it also says FINE CUISINE."

My personal culinary style and interpretation of Texas food reflects my passion for fine dining and Texas-style cooking. Texas has traditionally been known more for comfortable and casual food than for white linen tablecloth fare. In recent years, however, Texas has influenced the food scene of the entire nation with inventive and creative strides in the fine-dining arena. I chose the words "Fine Texas Cuisine" to describe my restaurant, because it defines exactly what we strive to provide. I'm passionate about fine cuisine, and I'm passionate about Texas heritage and Texas ingredients.

I began the concept for Bonnell's by researching Texas farms and ranches to find the highest quality and most unique ingredients. It wouldn't make sense to serve Georgia peaches when my neighboring county throws an annual festival dedicated to the peach-season harvest. I prefer the Parker County peaches that get to my door after only one trip in one truck to any produce sent via air, boat, or interstate. It's that intimate relationship with local food products that begins to *truly* define fine Texas cuisine.

Once the freshest farm ingredients are obtained in their peak of ripeness and freshness, my design work in the kitchen begins. My seasonings, flavors, and techniques come from those places I'm proud to call neighbors in a culinary sense. From our neighbors to the south, I borrow the Tex-Mex traditions that I grew up on, along with a few authentic Mexican tricks of the trade thrown in for good measure. From our easterly neighbors (past Dallas, of course), there will always be a special place in my heart for the New Orleans Creole flare that I picked up while working for the Brennan family in the French Quarter. I tend to bring a lot of southwestern ingredients into my kitchen as well, including various dried chiles and spice combinations. By borrowing a little inspiration from great neighbors, then applying it to farm-fresh ingredients that are Texas born and Texas bred, I've created my own brand of what customers now understand completely as "Fine Texas Cuisine." ★

# ★ ★ ★
# APPETIZERS

★ Venison Carpaccio with Green Peppercorn Dressing ★
★ Axis Venison Tartare ★
★ Buffalo-Style Frog Legs with Gorgonzola Dipping Sauce ★
★ Mesquite-Smoked Salmon Mousse ★
★ Smoked Buffalo and Black Pepper Boursin Roulades ★
★ Crispy Quail Legs with Southwestern Buttermilk Dressing ★
★ Goat Cheese and Crab-Stuffed Zucchini Blossoms in Beer Batter ★
★ Oysters Texasfeller ★ Pico D'Escargot ★ Rocky Mountain Elk Tacos ★
★ Smoked Buffalo Rib Empanadas ★ Smoked Tenderloin Nacho Tower ★
★ Texas Bruschetta ★ Wild Boar Chops with Peach Barbeque Sauce ★
★ Tequila-Flamed Quail and Grits ★

Without a doubt, appetizers are my favorite category on any menu, including the one in my own restaurant. When I arrive at any type of gathering, from a birthday party to a wedding, I can pretty much tell how the evening's going to go by the end of the first round of appetizers. It's the zone where chefs and hosts love to show off just a little bit. Anyone throwing a dinner party really sets the mood for the night with that first hors d'oeuvre tray or cocktail platter.

In the restaurant, customers seem to seek out the appetizers as a way to sample the chef's talent without the total commitment of choosing a full-size entrée. The most exciting thing about appetizers for a chef is the complete lack of rules, which leaves all options open. They don't have to have a vegetable, starch, sauce, or garnish. Appetizers are not supposed to fill someone up, although it's more than acceptable if they come close. With just a little tweaking, any dish that you can dream up can be shrunk down and fancied up to be the coolest, trendiest, most fashionable little canapé. On the appetizer page, we get the freedom to create one-biters, mini-size entrées, shooters, or exotic combinations with no creative limits. I recently cooked a dinner at the

James Beard House in New York City for some of the most discerning palates in the nation, and I started them off with barbecued pork sandwiches, miniaturized to fashionable bite-size cocktail portions, and rabbit loin corndogs. Carnival food can be elevated into fine dining, and sophisticated cuisine can become casual nuggets of comfort food when served properly as appetizers.

Since the portions are small, we can use any ingredient—no matter how rich, decadent, or rare—to create a little pearl of culinary mastery. Most diners are quick to sample things that only require a bite or two, even if they aren't sure of all the ingredients.

I've served over sixty different appetizers in my restaurant and countless more at dinner parties and casual get-togethers, but these are some tried-and-true Texas favorites that I come back to time after time. When people ask me what my favorite dish is, I usually say a sampling of every appetizer. Give me a big platter of small foods any day, and I'm a happy man. I can't remember the last time my father ever ordered anything from the entrée side of a menu. He's strictly an appetizer man. When it really comes down to it, I guess I am too. ★

*Mesquite-Smoked Salmon Mousse, recipe on page 20.*

# VENISON CARPACCIO WITH GREEN PEPPERCORN DRESSING

One of the purest ways to enjoy the flavor of venison is in a carpaccio preparation. I love the simplicity of this dish with the silky textured rare venison paired with tart and peppery flavors. **Serves 3 to 4**

---

**Dressing**
1 (3.5-ounce) can green
   peppercorns
Juice of 4 lemons
2 cups mayonnaise
2 cups sour cream
Zest of 2 lemons, chopped
7 tablespoons Dijon mustard
1 tablespoon Worcestershire
Salt and white pepper to taste

**Arugula**
1 pinch kosher salt
1 pinch white pepper
Juice of 1 lemon
1 teaspoon extra virgin olive oil
1 bunch fresh arugula

**Venison Carpaccio**
1 (6-ounce) axis venison backstrap,
   cleaned of all fat and connective
   tissue
1/2 teaspoon kosher salt
1/4 teaspoon ground black pepper
1/2 teaspoon canola oil
Caper berries, 3 per serving
Crispy fried capers, 6–8 per serving

**Green Peppercorn Dressing**
Purée the peppercorns with lemon juice in a food processor or blender. Combine with the remaining ingredients; set aside.

**Arugula**
Combine the seasonings, lemon juice, and oil in a mixing bowl and whisk together. Dress the arugula greens lightly with the vinaigrette just before plating.

**Venison Carpaccio**
Rub the venison on all sides with salt and pepper, then sear in canola oil in a very hot pan just until the venison gets a light brown color on all sides. The meat should remain raw inside. Remove from the pan and wrap tightly in plastic wrap and freeze. After the venison is frozen solid, remove the plastic wrap and slice extremely thin, using an electric slicer. (If you don't have an electric slicer, skip the freezing step; thinly slice the meat with a sharp knife and gently pound thin between two sheets of plastic wrap.) Cover a dinner plate with one even layer of the thinly sliced meat and allow to thaw. This should take about 1 to 2 minutes. Place a few of the dressed arugula greens in the center of the plate, drizzle with the peppercorn dressing, and garnish with a few caper berries and crispy fried capers.

---

# AXIS VENISON TARTARE

★ ★ ★

Venison is some of the best suited meat (and one of the safest) for tartare preparations because it's extremely flavorful and lean. This is a great way to bring back an old classic dish with bold new flavor and style. **Serves 2**

**Pico de Gallo**
1 small onion, diced
2 Roma tomatoes, diced
1 large jalapeño, diced
2 tablespoons lime juice
1 tablespoon chopped cilantro

**Venison**
$1/2$ shallot, minced
1 tablespoon finely diced tomato
1 tablespoon capers
$1/2$ clove garlic, minced
Juice of $1/4$ lemon
1 teaspoon Dijon mustard
1–2 dashes hot sauce
1–2 dashes Worcestershire sauce
$1/2$ teaspoon chopped cilantro
1 pinch kosher salt
1 pinch ground black pepper
4–6 ounces venison (lean meat only), cleaned and trimmed
1 ripe avocado
Arugula leaves, as garnish

**Pico de Gallo**
Combine all ingredients; set aside.

**Venison**
Mix all ingredients together except for the venison, avocado, and arugula. Arrange the avocado in slices around the inside of a ring mold. Dice the venison into very small cubes. Mix 2 tablespoons diced venison with 2 tablespoons of the other mixture. Spoon the mixture into the center of the avocado-lined ring mold and then carefully slide off the ring. Garnish with arugula leaves and Pico de Gallo. Serve immediately with toast points or crostini. This dish can also be served on spoons or forks individually as a passed appetizer.

★ **TIP:** The venison must be cubed and mixed with the other ingredients just prior to serving. Do not prepare too far ahead of time. The other ingredients can be mixed a day ahead of time and kept in the refrigerator. Serve the dish within a few minutes of the final preparation. It will not taste the same or have the same texture after about 15 minutes.

# BUFFALO-STYLE FROG LEGS WITH GORGONZOLA DIPPING SAUCE

Frog legs are a real Texas treat. The texture lies somewhere between fish and chicken, but the flavor is succulent and unique. By starting off with the familiar flavors of buffalo wings, this becomes a great recipe for introducing frog legs to someone who might not be familiar with them. Once you get someone hooked on the tender and juicy nature of fresh frog legs, you just might have a hard time getting them to eat chicken again. **Serves 3 to 4**

---

**Dipping Sauce**
1/3 cup plus 2 tablespoons crumbled
  Gorgonzola cheese
1/2 cup mayonnaise
1/2 cup sour cream
1 dash Worcestershire sauce
1 dash Tabasco sauce
1/4 teaspoon kosher salt
1 pinch ground white pepper

**Frog Legs**
12 large frog legs
1 1/2 cups buttermilk
6 tablespoons Frank's RedHot
  Original Cayenne Pepper Sauce,
  divided
2 cups flour
3 tablespoons Bonnell's Creole
  Seasoning Blend (page 182)
2 quarts canola oil

**Gorgonzola Dipping Sauce**
Combine all ingredients together and chill until ready to use.

**Buffalo-Style Frog Legs**
Marinate the frog legs in buttermilk and 3 tablespoons hot sauce overnight in the refrigerator. Pull the frog legs from the buttermilk and immediately dredge in a mixture of the flour and Creole seasoning. Coat well on all sides, then deep-fry in 365-degree F oil for 2 to 3 minutes, or until the legs are golden brown on the outside and cooked through. The fryer time may vary slightly, depending on the size of the frog legs. You can usually tell that they are done when they float and almost stop bubbling in the oil. Be sure to turn them over at least once while frying to ensure they cook on all sides.

Place remaining hot sauce in a large mixing bowl and drop in the frog legs as soon as they come out of the fryer. Toss them in the hot sauce a few times, and then serve with the dipping sauce.

---

# MESQUITE-SMOKED SALMON MOUSSE

I love to serve this as a dip with Belgian endive leaves arranged like chips for scooping. You can substitute smoked salmon that's already prepared if you want an easy shortcut, but smoking the salmon over mesquite really adds a unique flavor. For any sportsman who just returned from an Alaskan trip, this is a great way to utilize that wild catch for your next party. **Serves 10 to 12** *(photo on page 13)*

6 ounces fresh wild salmon

1/2 cup plus 2 tablespoons cream cheese

1/4 cup heavy cream

1 small shallot, diced

2 tablespoons chopped fresh dill

Juice of 1 lemon

1/4 teaspoon kosher salt

1 Belgian endive, red or white or a combination

Dill sprigs or capers for garnish

Smoke the salmon over mesquite wood until an internal temperature of 140 degrees F is reached. Skin the salmon and be sure all bones have been removed. Cool completely and then combine with all remaining ingredients except endive and dill capers in a food processor. Mix until smooth. This mousse can be placed in a pastry bag and piped onto the leaves of the Belgian endive to use as a passed appetizer, or it can be served in a bowl with endive leaves for dipping. Garnish with fresh dill sprigs or capers.

# SMOKED BUFFALO AND BLACK PEPPER BOURSIN ROULADES

I love the flavor combination of smoky, rich buffalo meat with creamy, peppery Boursin cheese in this dish. The presentation is not hard to pull off, but it will make you look like a pro. **Serves 8 to 10**

---

**2 pounds buffalo tenderloin**
**1 tablespoon Bonnell's Creole**
**Seasoning Blend (page 182)**
**2 (5-ounce) boxes Boursin Black**
**Pepper Cheese**

Rub the tenderloin with the seasoning and let sit for 1 hour in the refrigerator. Preheat oven to 400 degrees F.

Roast tenderloin until internal temperature reaches 125 degrees F. Remove from the oven and let rest 5 minutes; wrap in plastic, and allow to cool completely. Cover a smooth counter surface with overlapping sheets of plastic wrap. Slice the tenderloin very thin and form a large rectangle with slightly overlapping pieces of buffalo on the plastic wrap. Warm the Boursin lightly in the microwave for just a few seconds to make smooth. Carefully spread the cheese over the entire surface of buffalo, then use the wrap to roll tightly like a jellyroll. Refrigerate at least 1 hour, wrapped tightly in plastic. This can also be refrigerated overnight; it will keep up to 2 days in the refrigerator. Remove from refrigerator, slice into roulades, and remove the plastic from each slice; place roulades on thinly sliced, toasted French bread crostinis.

---

# CRISPY QUAIL LEGS WITH SOUTHWESTERN BUTTERMILK DRESSING

I discovered this dish by accident. When I first contacted Diamond H Ranch and asked them for a sample of the quail products that they produce, I was quite surprised to find a package of just legs in the box. I fried them quickly just to try them and then watched in astonishment as my wife and best friend put away the first batch of twenty and pleaded for more. Quail legs have become one of my true signature dishes since then. This dish can also be done with wild quail, but the taste will not be nearly the same as the birds being produced by my friends at Diamond H down in Bandera. They have been working for years with Texas A&M University to breed and produce the finest quail in the world. As much as I enjoy the wild bobwhites, I have to admit that the farm-raised quail from these guys are by far the best tasting. **Serves 4**

---

### Quail Legs
20 quail legs, cleaned,
   thigh bone removed (we like
   Diamond H Ranch)
1 cup buttermilk
3 tablespoons hot sauce
1 cup flour
3 tablespoons Bonnell's Creole
   Seasoning Blend (page 182)
2 quarts canola oil

### Dressing
1/2 cup buttermilk
1/2 cup mayonnaise
2 tablespoons sour cream
1 teaspoon dried parsley flakes
1/2 teaspoon ground black pepper
1/3 teaspoon salt
1 teaspoon garlic powder
1/2 teaspoon chopped chives
   (dry or fresh)
1/2 teaspoon onion powder
1/4 teaspoon dried thyme
1 pinch cayenne pepper
2 teaspoons Bonnell's Creole
   Seasoning Blend (page 182)
Crystal Hot Sauce (start with 4–6
   dashes), to taste

### Crispy Quail Legs
Rinse the quail legs and soak in a mixture of buttermilk and hot sauce for at least 2 hours. This can be done a full day ahead of time. Mix the flour and seasoning, and dredge the legs in the dry mixture. Be sure to coat the legs well on all sides in the flour before frying. Bring canola oil to 375 degrees F, deep-fry the legs for approximately 2 minutes, and then drain on paper towels. Serve with the dressing on the side for dipping.

### Southwestern Buttermilk Dressing
Whisk all ingredients together and chill for at least 30 minutes. Adjust with more hot sauce if desired.

---

# GOAT CHEESE AND CRAB-STUFFED ZUCCHINI BLOSSOMS IN BEER BATTER

★　★　★

This is a true Texas delicacy to share with great friends. Squash blossoms have a sweet and delicate flavor, but they are one of the most perishable ingredients you can buy. When they are in season, grab 'em and use 'em quickly. The succulent flavor of fresh crab tucked inside these special flowers with a light crispy batter oozing with soft cheese is just a thing of beauty. There is definitely some labor involved in making this dish work, but the rewards are well worth the trouble. **Serves 4**

---

1 teaspoon fresh basil
1/2 teaspoon fresh thyme
1 teaspoon fresh dill
1/2 teaspoon fresh cilantro
8 ounces fresh goat cheese
3/4 teaspoon salt, divided,
　　plus more to taste
1 pinch ground black pepper
8 ounces jumbo lump wild blue
　　crabmeat
12 large zucchini blossoms
1 cup flour
1 (12-ounce) bottle cold light beer

Remove and discard the stems from all fresh herbs; finely chop herbs. Combine the herbs, goat cheese, 1/2 teaspoon salt and the pepper until smooth, then place in a pastry bag (or use a ziplock bag and cut off one corner if you don't have a pastry bag). Pick through the crabmeat for any shell pieces and then carefully place one or two big pieces of crabmeat inside each zucchini blossom. Pipe in the goat cheese mixture until the flower is filled. Refrigerate for at least 15 minutes.

Combine the flour and remaining salt together in a large mixing bowl and then slowly pour in the beer while whisking until the batter reaches the proper consistency. The exact amount of beer needed will vary with different types of flour, but watch for the right consistency more than anything. It should be a little lighter than pancake batter—just barely thick enough to coat the blossoms when they are dipped in, but not watery to the point where it all just runs right off. This is meant to be a very light crispy coating on the outside of the blossoms, not a heavy, thick beer batter.

Dip the blossoms in the beer batter and quickly drop in a deep fryer at 375 degrees F. Fry just until the outside becomes crispy, about 1 to 2 minutes, then immediately drain on paper towels. Lightly salt the blossoms when they come out of the fryer and serve immediately. It may be necessary to turn the blossoms over in the oil while frying to get them cooked on all sides.

---

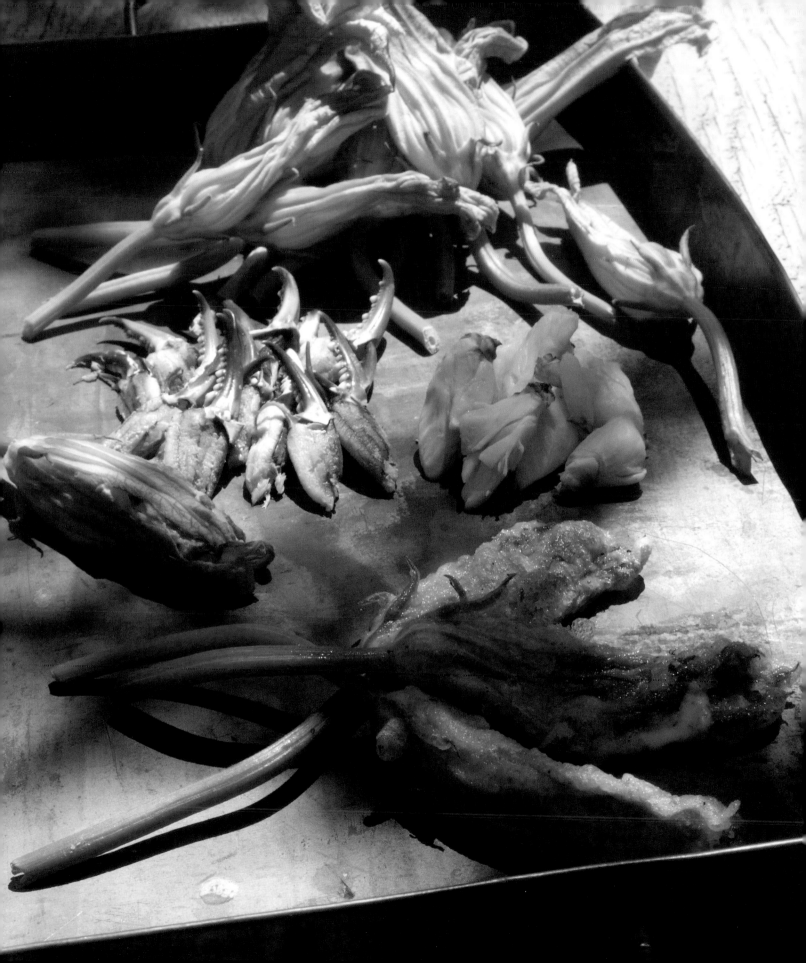

# OYSTERS TEXASFELLER

If I did have one personal favorite dish, which I'm not admitting to, this would probably be it. That old rule about good oysters only being available in months with an "r" was written in the late 1700s and no longer applies. Someone somewhere is harvesting fresh beautiful oysters every single day of the year. I love the Galveston Bay oysters for this dish because of their plump and juicy size, and I can get them really fresh, but any good-quality oyster will work. I can't even count the number of guests who at one time "didn't like oysters" but now come back regularly for their Texasfeller fix. The tangy brine flavor of fresh oysters nestled in a light crispy coating with spicy tasso, wilted spinach, and velvety hollandaise is a combination that gets people hooked for life. When anyone asks what the chef recommends, my answer always starts with the question "Do *you* like oysters?" **Serves 3 to 4**

12 Galveston Bay Oysters (live)
$^2/_3$ cup buttermilk
1 tablespoon Crystal Hot Sauce
1 cup flour
2 tablespoons Bonnell's Creole
   Seasoning Blend (page 182)
2 quarts canola oil
1 shallot, minced
1 clove garlic, minced
1 teaspoon butter
3 ounces tasso ham, diced
2 cups chopped fresh spinach
1 bunch cilantro, chopped
1 pinch kosher salt
1 tablespoon dry white wine

Hollandaise Sauce
3 egg yolks
$1^1/_2$ tablespoons dry white wine
1 teaspoon hot sauce
$1^1/_2$ teaspoons lemon juice
1 pinch cayenne pepper
$^1/_2$ teaspoon salt
1 cup clarified butter

Clean the shells, shuck the oysters, and remove from shells. Discard only the top halves of the oyster shells. Marinate the oysters in a mixture of buttermilk and hot sauce for at least 2 hours in the refrigerator. This can be done overnight; but they must be kept cold. Dredge the oysters in a mixture of flour and seasoning until well coated. Fry the oysters in 375-degree F oil for approximately 1 to 2 minutes. Drain on paper towels.

Over medium heat, sweat the shallot and garlic in butter in a sauté pan. Add the tasso, then top with spinach and cilantro, and season with salt. Splash in the wine and cook just until the spinach is wilted. To be safe, the oyster shells can be boiled before using. Fill each shell with the spinach mixture, then place one oyster on top of each and spoon a silky layer of Hollandaise Sauce over the top.

### Hollandaise Sauce
Slowly cook egg yolks, wine, and hot sauce over a double boiler while whisking. When the yolks have doubled in volume, add remaining ingredients except for the butter. Slowly drizzle the butter in while whisking vigorously. Season with additional salt to taste. Store in a warm place until ready to use. Do not refrigerate or reheat. This is a very unstable sauce that must be served immediately.

# PICO D'ESCARGOT

I've always loved escargot, ever since my parents had me try one at age five without telling me what it was. But I always wondered why there only seemed to be one way of serving them. As much as I love the idea of bubbling garlic butter and herbs, the chef in me likes to experiment and play around with ingredients. This recipe is simply a sauté of pico de gallo with escargot and a touch of cream to hold everything together. This dish is a fun way to put a little Texas twist on a traditional French ingredient. **Serves 2**

1 teaspoon olive oil
1 shallot, minced
16 snails (canned), drained and rinsed
1 jalapeño pepper, seeded and diced
¼ teaspoon salt
½ teaspoon ground black pepper
1 clove garlic, minced
2 Roma tomatoes, seeded and diced
Splash of dry white wine
Juice of 1 lime
⅓ cup heavy cream
1 cup cooked white rice
3–4 fresh cilantro sprigs, chopped

Heat a medium-size sauté pan, and then add olive oil, shallot, snails, and jalapeño. Season lightly with salt and pepper, and sweat until the shallot becomes translucent; add the garlic and tomatoes. Deglaze the pan with wine. Allow the wine to reduce until the pan is almost dry. Add the lime juice and heavy cream, and simmer until the cream thickens. Adjust seasonings and serve over white rice. Garnish with cilantro just before serving.

# ROCKY MOUNTAIN ELK TACOS

This is the number one most popular appetizer I've ever served. You can literally see folks' eyes light up at a fancy party when a tray of cute little tacos comes by for them to sample. But they are far different from any taco you've ever tasted. They work just fine as a full-size taco for casual fare, but the mini-size portions are always a huge hit with crowds. Taco shells are easy to make and always taste better when they are fried fresh. To make the mini versions, cut a round circle out of a corn tortilla with a cookie cutter and fry the same as you would a large taco shell. Serves 12 to 14

---

5 pounds lean elk meat,
    cleaned of any silverskin, fat, or
    connective tissue
1 (2½-ounce) can chipotle peppers in
    adobo sauce
½ bunch fresh cilantro
3 cloves garlic
1 medium white potato, peeled and
    cut into small cubes
3 shallots
1 jalapeño, seeded and diced
5 fresh Roma tomatoes, chopped
1 teaspoon kosher salt
¼ teaspoon ground black pepper
50 corn tortillas
8 ounces queso fresco, grated
Pico de Gallo, as garnish (page 16)

This recipe takes two days to prepare. On the first day, cut the elk meat into medium-size chunks. Purée the chipotles (entire contents of can), cilantro, and garlic in a food processor. Pour the mixture over the elk cubes and cover with plastic wrap. Allow to marinate overnight in the refrigerator.

On the second day, using the fine plate on a meat grinder, grind the elk meat with all of the marinade. Boil the potato cubes in a separate pot, then strain off the water.

In a large pot, brown the shallots, jalapeño, and elk meat until cooked through, then add tomatoes and potatoes, and simmer lightly for 15 to 20 minutes. Adjust the seasonings as needed and serve in taco shells with Green Chile Cheese Grits (page 176). Garnish with queso fresco and Pico de Gallo.

---

# SMOKED BUFFALO RIB EMPANADAS

Empanadas are what some Texans call fried pies. They can be made into any size and garnished more ways than I can count. Usually, I like to serve the bigger ones for casual home-cooked meals and the smaller versions for fancier events like cocktail parties. **Serves 10 to 12 as appetizers or 4 to 6 as entrées**

**Dough**
2 tablespoons shortening
1 egg plus 2 egg yolks
1/2 cup milk
2 cups flour
1 teaspoon baking powder
1/2 teaspoon salt

**Filling**
2 pounds buffalo short ribs
2 tablespoons Bonnell's Creole
   Seasoning Blend (page 182)
1 cup chicken stock
1 (12-ounce) can chopped tomatoes

**Dough**
Preheat oven to 350 degrees F.

Place all ingredients except the 2 egg yolks into a large mixing bowl and combine by hand gently, just until the dough is a uniform texture. Be sure the egg is evenly distributed, but do not knead or over mix.

Liberally flour a smooth kitchen surface and roll out the dough to approximately 1/8 to 1/4 inch thick. Cut into circles with any size round cookie cutter. Brush the outer edge with a little egg yolk, place a spoonful of the filling in the center, and then fold the circle over to form a little pocket. Use the tines of a fork to gently seal the edges. Lightly brush the tops with the egg yolk and garnish with extra pieces of the dough for a fancier look. Bake until tops are golden brown and slightly crisp, about 20 minutes. Serve with Guajillo Chile Sauce (page 84) for dipping.

**Filling**
Rub the short ribs generously with seasoning and smoke in a 225-degree F pecan wood smoker for 2 hours. Remove the short ribs and place in a small Dutch oven with the stock and tomatoes. Cover with a tight-fitting lid and cook in an oven at 250 degrees F for 4 hours, until the meat just falls off the bone. Remove the buffalo meat and cut into small cubes. Use some of the braising liquid to keep it moist when stuffing the empanadas.

# SMOKED TENDERLOIN NACHO TOWER

This is the perfect kind of appetizer to serve at football parties when you want to impress the guys. It's a chip-and-dip dish taken to a completely new level. The size of your tower will completely depend on the size of your ring mold. Be careful not to construct a tower that is too tall to stand. A big sour cream container with the bottom cut off can be used to make a larger tower, or all of the ingredients can be mixed together and placed on chips individually for a passed nacho appetizer with a drizzle of sour cream for garnish. **Serves 6 to 8**

---

12 ounces beef tenderloin
1 tablespoon Bonnell's Southwestern
   Seasoning Blend (page 181)
12 flour tortillas
½ cup plus 2 tablespoons
   guacamole (see below)
3 tablespoons chopped scallions
2 tablespoons chopped fresh
   cilantro
½ cup sour cream
½ cup Pico de Gallo (page 16)
Freshly fried flour tortilla chips, for
   garnish

Guacamole
2 large ripe avocados
1 large jalapeño
1 clove garlic
2 teaspoons chopped cilantro
1 tablespoon lime juice
Salt and pepper

Season the tenderloin well with seasoning and smoke in a pecan wood smoker until the internal temperature reaches 135 degrees F. Remove the meat, wrap tightly in plastic, and refrigerate.

Cut the tortillas into triangles, fry at 350 degrees F until crispy, and then dry on paper towels. Lightly salt as soon as they come out of the hot oil. Begin the presentation by placing a ring mold (or a 2 to 3-inch piece of PVC pipe) in the center of a plate. Unwrap the tenderloin and dice into small cubes, then place a layer inside the ring mold. Pack down firmly with the handle of a knife, then add a layer of guacamole on top of the meat, followed by scallions, cilantro, sour cream, and Pico de Gallo. It may help to tap the plate against the table a few times to help pack down the ingredients while holding the ring mold to keep it from tipping over. Just before serving, carefully remove the ring and garnish with the freshly fried flour tortilla chips.

### Guacamole
Mix all ingredients together in a blender or food processor. For less heat, remove jalapeño seeds first. Season with salt and pepper to taste.

---

# TEXAS BRUSCHETTA

This dish has pretty much nothing to do with the traditional Italian bruschetta, so it's quite appropriate that most people even mispronounce the name. It is a fun dish to share with friends, though, and the flavors mix together in some really interesting ways. To appreciate the complexity of each of the flavors, try topping a chip with all four of the dips mixed together for a mouthwatering explosion of taste. Be as creative as you like with the presentation. I like to think of this dish as the ultimate chip and dip platter. **Serves 8 to 10**

---

**Goat Cheese**
8 ounces goat cheese (I like Deborah's Farmstead)
1 teaspoon chopped basil
1 teaspoon chopped thyme
1/2 tablespoon chopped dill
1/2 tablespoon chopped cilantro
1/2 teaspoon salt
1 1/2 teaspoons fresh goat's milk
1 pinch ground black pepper

**Relish**
2 ripe Hass avocados
1 clove garlic
1/2 jalapeño, seeded
3-4 cilantro sprigs
Juice of 1/2 lime
1/4 teaspoon kosher salt
1 cup pecan halves
1 1/2 teaspoons olive oil
2 teaspoons Bonnell's Creole Seasoning Blend (page 182)

**Salsa**
2 Roma tomatoes, peeled if desired
1 small onion
1 large jalapeño, halved and seeds removed
1/4 teaspoon salt
Pepper
Juice of 1 lime
4-5 cilantro sprigs, chopped

**Onions**
1 large Texas 1015 onion
2 teaspoons canola oil
Pinch of salt
Pinch of freshly ground black pepper

**Chips**
10 large flour tortillas

**Fresh Herb Goat Cheese**
Combine all ingredients; set aside.

**Avocado and Pecan Relish**
Preheat oven to 350 degrees F. Combine first 6 ingredients in a food processor and pulse until smooth. Toss the pecans, olive oil, and seasoning in a mixing bowl and combine well. Place avocado mixture on a baking sheet and bake until toasted, about 5 to 7 minutes. Chop seasoned pecans and place on top of avocado mixture.

**Fire-Roasted Salsa**
Grill the tomatoes, onion, and jalapeño until slightly charred on all sides. Roughly chop or pulse in a food processor. Season with salt and pepper, add lime juice and cilantro, and chill. If keeping for more than 1 hour, and wait to add the salt until ready to serve.

**Caramelized Texas 1015 Onions**
Cut onion into julienne strips and caramelize in a nonstick pan with canola oil until lightly browned. Season lightly with salt and pepper.

**Flour Tortilla Chips**
Cut flour tortillas into triangles and fry until golden brown. Season with salt as soon as the chips come out of the oil. Drain on paper towels.

Arrange each of the components on a plate or large serving platter and serve with tortilla chips.

---

# WILD BOAR CHOPS WITH PEACH BARBEQUE SAUCE

Wild boars (feral hogs, to be exact) in Texas are nothing more than domestic pigs that got out a while back and have being living in the wild for several generations. Living on a natural diet and getting exercise makes the meat leaner and very rich in flavor. They are a nuisance to ranchers and can be terribly destructive, but their meat is exceptional. Even folks who might never order wild boar from a menu will find it hard to resist these little appetizing chops. **Serves 5 to 6**

---

**Wild Boar Chops**

2 whole frenched racks of Texas wild boar (I use Frontier Meats)

1/2 cup Bonnell's Southwestern Seasoning Blend (page 181)

**Barbecue Sauce**

1 sweet onion, diced

6 tablespoons butter

4 local fresh peaches, pitted

3 ancho chiles, stemmed and seeded

1 1/2 cups ketchup

1/2 bunch cilantro, diced

6 tablespoons brown sugar

1/3 cup bourbon

Juice of 1 lime

2 cups chicken stock

1/4 teaspoon kosher salt

1 pinch ground black pepper

**Wild Boar Chops**

Clean the racks of wild boar of any sinew and excess fat. Rub generously with seasoning and allow to sit for at least 45 minutes. Grill over mesquite coals on medium heat until an internal temperature of 140 to 145 degrees F is reached. Do not overcook or the boar will become very dry. Allow to rest for about 10 minutes before cutting into chops. Arrange the individual chops around a bowl of barbecue sauce and serve.

**Peach Barbecue Sauce**

Sauté the onion in butter until soft. Add all remaining ingredients and bring to a simmer. Allow to simmer lightly for 20 to 25 minutes. Purée with a stick blender until smooth. If the sauce is too thin, reduce by simmering longer. If it's too thick, add a touch more bourbon.

---

# TEQUILA-FLAMED QUAIL AND GRITS

I use quail in more ways than I can count at the restaurant. When I had a little extra quail meat on hand one day, I came up with a way to prepare the quail pieces with the sweetness of tequila. Chef Ed McOwen then suggested pairing the quail stew with our grits for an appetizer served in a skillet. It became an instant success. **Serves 3 to 4**

## Grits
1 roasted poblano pepper, chopped
½ cup chopped onion
1 teaspoon chopped garlic
1 teaspoon butter
1 cup heavy cream
1 cup chicken stock
Salt and pepper, to taste
Bonnell's Creole Seasoning Blend,
    to taste (page 182)
½ cup Homestead Gristmill Stone
    Ground Grits
¼ cup grated cheddar cheese
¼ cup grated jack cheese

## Quail
6 ounces boneless quail meat,
    cleaned and diced
2 tablespoons olive oil
Salt and pepper, to taste
1 shallot, diced
1 poblano pepper, roasted, peeled,
    and seeded
1 clove garlic
2 tablespoons diced red pepper
1 serrano chile, diced
¼ cup chicken stock
2 tablespoons Gold Tequila
Pico de Gallo, to garnish (page 16)
Queso fresco, to garnish
Freshly fried flour tortilla chips,
    for serving

### Green Chile Cheese Grits
Sauté the chile, onion, and garlic in butter until soft. Add cream and stock and bring to a simmer (the stage just before a rolling boil). Be careful not to let the liquids boil over. Quickly whisk in seasonings and grits. Stir constantly until grits begin to thicken. This should take about 15 to 20 minutes. Gently fold in cheeses and let sit for at least 5 minutes.

### Tequila-Glazed Quail
In a hot nonstick skillet, brown the quail meat in olive oil, then season with salt and pepper. Add the remaining solid ingredients and cook until soft. Deglaze with stock and reduce by half.

Add tequila and allow to flame. (NEVER pour alcohol straight from the bottle; pour from a separate glass.)

Fill a serving dish with grits and then top with quail, Pico de Gallo, and queso fresco. Serve with flour tortilla chips.

# SOUPS AND SALADS

★ ★ ★

★ Chilled Brandywine Tomato Soup with Mesquite-Smoked Salmon ★
★ Creamy Avocado Soup ★ Grilled Quail Salad ★
★ Grilled Tomato and Mozzarella Salad with Cilantro Pesto ★
★ Gulf Shrimp and Crab-Stuffed Avocado ★
★ Lobster and Cantaloupe Salad with Truffle Dressing ★
★ Roasted Tomato and Jalapeño Soup ★
★ Roasted Red Pepper and Grilled Corn Chowder ★
★ Chili-Rubbed Smoked Antelope Salad with Crispy Tobacco Onion Rings ★
★ Vodka Gazpacho ★ White Gazpacho ★ Wild Mushroom and Duck Gumbo ★
★ Wilted Spinach Salad with Blue Crab, Chilied Pecans, and Warm Bacon Vinaigrette ★
★ Lemon Caesar Salad with Southwestern Croutons ★

---

Soup and salad have always played a major role in the Texas food scene. In the middle of a hot Texas summer, a cool bowl of gazpacho and a spicy salad can be the perfect lunch for the workingman, while in the winter it may turn into a rich tomato and jalapeño soup with a spinach salad tossed with crabmeat and warm bacon vinaigrette. In the midday hour, soups and salads are king, and the sky is the limit when it comes to different varieties of each. It's truly a sign of love when someone goes the extra mile to make homemade soup and salad dressing from scratch rather than open a can or bottle. This is comfort food at its core, but it can also be fine dining when just the right amount of know-how and proper technique is applied.

For all-out comfort food, nothing speaks to my soul like soup. I can still remember the exact smell of the house when Mom would make homemade tomato soup, and how the vapors would fill every corner of every room as the big, red, weathered Dutch oven simmered away for hours. Soup tends to bring back childhood memories for almost everyone. I can't really think of an exact definition for soup, because it's such a broad category of things. Soups can be rich and meaty, hot and spicy, cool and creamy, or thick and chunky. Even a consommé, which is clear and thin, can have intense flavors. The only rule I have for soup is that it needs flavor—intense, rich flavor. Even cold soups can raise an eyebrow on most Texans if they have enough bold flavor.

Salad always starts with the freshest produce possible. There's simply no comparison between lettuce in a preportioned bag from an average supermarket and farm-fresh baby greens from a farmers market or from the garden. And don't forget the homegrown tomatoes; they are one of my greatest loves in the entire world. Simply starting with the freshest farm ingredients gets you halfway home when creating the perfect salad. Learning how to make great salad dressing from scratch is another sign that you truly care about your family members or guests. It's a labor of love. Most people won't expect much out of a salad course—I guess we tend to think it's going to be the same old thing. But when you get someone to look up in amazement and really comment on how great that salad turned out, you know that you've created something special. I think it's fun to get a little creative—like stuffing a perfectly ripe Texas cantaloupe with succulent lobster salad—and turn the salad course into the main event of the meal. ★

*Roasted Tomato and Jalapeño Soup, recipe on page 54.*

# CHILLED BRANDYWINE TOMATO SOUP WITH MESQUITE-SMOKED SALMON

When it's tomato season in Texas, you simply can't have too many recipes for tomato soup. This is one of the best ways to make use of tomatoes that might be ultra-ripe but just a little too soft to serve sliced. The quality of this soup will depend 100 percent on the quality of the tomatoes. Mesquite-smoked salmon adds an outstanding flavor combination to this dish, but it's easy to shortcut by buying smoked salmon as well. **Serves 4**

---

### Soup
1 large sweet onion, chopped
3 teaspoons extra virgin olive oil, divided
1½ teaspoons kosher salt
1 pinch white pepper
3 cloves garlic, minced
Splash of dry white wine
4 large Brandywine tomatoes, cut into rough pieces
3–4 fresh basil leaves, julienned
Juice from 1 lemon

### Salmon
¼ cup kosher salt
2 tablespoons brown sugar
2 tablespoons sugar
6 ounces fresh wild salmon
6–8 fresh dill sprigs
1 tablespoon nonpareil capers (if you use larger capers, chop them up)

### Chilled Brandywine Tomato Soup
In a large soup pot, lightly sauté the onion in 2 teaspoons olive oil until soft. Season with salt and pepper. When onion looks almost clear, add the garlic. Sweat for another minute, add wine, and then reduce mixture until the pot is almost dry. Add the tomatoes, including any juices, and simmer for 15 minutes, stirring occasionally. Add basil and purée with a stick blender. Drizzle in remaining olive oil while blending to give the soup a richer feel. Check for seasonings and then chill the soup. After the soup has been chilled, add lemon juice and taste again for seasonings, as they can vary in different temperatures. The soup can be served as is, or strained for a more upscale look and feel.

### Mesquite-Smoked Salmon
Mix the salt and sugars together, and coat the fish completely in the mixture. Let sit overnight in the refrigerator, packed in this cure. Thoroughly rinse the salmon the next day and allow to dry. Place in a cold smoker with dill on top and allow to cold smoke (not over 55 degrees F) over mesquite chips for 1 hour. Remove, wrap tightly in plastic wrap, and chill. Once the salmon has chilled, remove from plastic, remove the dill, then finely dice the salmon. Combine with remaining dill and capers. Add the salmon mixture to a shallow soup bowl, using a ring mold to keep it in the center. Top with a small frond of dill or chives for garnish; pour the chilled soup around the sides. This can be done tableside with a small pitcher for a stunning presentation.

---

# CREAMY AVOCADO SOUP

This dish is pure hedonism. This isn't for those on a diet, but it is rich and decadent in every way and a great dish for special occasions. **Serves 4**

2 shallots, finely diced
1 fresh jalapeño, seeded and chopped
1 clove garlic, chopped
2 tablespoons butter
1 (12-ounce) can tomatoes, drained and finely diced
1 cup chicken stock
1¹/₂ cups cream
¹/₄ teaspoon kosher salt
1 pinch white pepper
Juice from ¹/₂ lime
2 tablespoons chopped fresh cilantro
2 ripe avocados, diced into large cubes

In a saucepan, sauté the shallots, jalapeño, and garlic in butter until soft. Add the tomatoes and liquids. Season with salt and pepper and simmer for 10 to 15 minutes. Add the lime juice, cilantro, and avocado. Check for seasonings and serve.

# ROCKY MOUNTAIN ELK TACOS

This is the number one most popular appetizer I've ever served. You can literally see folks' eyes light up at a fancy party when a tray of cute little tacos comes by for them to sample. But they are far different from any taco you've ever tasted. They work just fine as a full-size taco for casual fare, but the mini-size portions are always a huge hit with crowds. Taco shells are easy to make and always taste better when they are fried fresh. To make the mini versions, cut a round circle out of a corn tortilla with a cookie cutter and fry the same as you would a large taco shell.
Serves 12 to 14

---

5 pounds lean elk meat,
  cleaned of any silverskin, fat, or
  connective tissue
1 (2½-ounce) can chipotle peppers in
  adobo sauce
½ bunch fresh cilantro
3 cloves garlic
1 medium white potato, peeled and
  cut into small cubes
3 shallots
1 jalapeño, seeded and diced
5 fresh Roma tomatoes, chopped
1 teaspoon kosher salt
¼ teaspoon ground black pepper
50 corn tortillas
8 ounces queso fresco, grated
Pico de Gallo, as garnish (page 16)

This recipe takes two days to prepare. On the first day, cut the elk meat into medium-size chunks. Purée the chipotles (entire contents of can), cilantro, and garlic in a food processor. Pour the mixture over the elk cubes and cover with plastic wrap. Allow to marinate overnight in the refrigerator.

On the second day, using the fine plate on a meat grinder, grind the elk meat with all of the marinade. Boil the potato cubes in a separate pot, then strain off the water.

In a large pot, brown the shallots, jalapeño, and elk meat until cooked through, then add tomatoes and potatoes, and simmer lightly for 15 to 20 minutes. Adjust the seasonings as needed and serve in taco shells with Green Chile Cheese Grits (page 176). Garnish with queso fresco and Pico de Gallo.

---

# GRILLED QUAIL SALAD

This salad is the perfect size for lunch. The grilled quail brings about 4–5 ounces of protein to a rich salad that combines just the right balance of sweetness and spice. **Serves 2**

---

**2 semi-boneless large quail (we like those from Diamond H Ranch)**
**3–4 fresh thyme sprigs**
**1 fresh rosemary sprig**
**2 cloves garlic**
**2½ tablespoons olive oil, divided**
**2½ teaspoons Bonnell's Creole Seasoning Blend, divided (page 182)**
**½ cup pecan halves**
**Fresh mixed baby greens**
**Southwestern Buttermilk Dressing (page 22)**
**16–20 dried cherries**
**4 hard-boiled quail eggs (we like those from Diamond H Ranch)**

Marinate the quail overnight in a mixture of the fresh herbs, garlic, and 2 tablespoons olive oil. Sprinkle the birds with 1 teaspoon seasoning and grill over medium to high heat until golden brown and cooked through. If necessary, finish in a 375-degree F oven rather than cook completely on the grill.

Toss the pecans, remaining olive oil, and remaining seasoning in a mixing bowl until well combined. Bake at 350 degrees F until toasted, about 5 to 7 minutes. Roughly chop the pecans.

Toss the baby greens with Southwestern Buttermilk Dressing and top with dried cherries, toasted pecans, and a grilled quail. Slice the hard-boiled quail eggs in half and serve alongside.

---

# GRILLED TOMATO AND MOZZARELLA SALAD WITH CILANTRO PESTO

I grew up on tomato and mozzarella salad, but this particular version is now my favorite. Grilling the tomatoes and toasting the cheese adds a richness to this dish that's hard to beat, and drizzling with a rich pesto puts this dish over the top in terms of intense flavor. **Serves 2**

---

### Pesto
2 tablespoons pine nuts
1 bunch fresh basil, leaves only
1 bunch fresh cilantro, leaves only
1 tablespoon grated Parmesan cheese
1 anchovy fillet
1 small clove garlic
Juice of 1 lemon
½ teaspoon salt
½ cup plus 2 tablespoons extra virgin olive oil

### Salad
2 ripe tomatoes
Salt and pepper, to taste
1–2 teaspoons extra virgin olive oil
2 (4-ounce) balls fresh mozzarella cheese
½ teaspoon aged balsamic vinegar
4–6 basil or cilantro leaves, for garnish

### Cilantro Pesto
Lightly toast the pine nuts in a small nonstick pan over medium heat until just lightly browned on all sides. Place all ingredients into a blender except for the olive oil. While blending, slowly drizzle in the olive oil until a thick sauce is achieved. Adjust the thickness of the pesto by adding or subtracting different amounts of oil.

### Grilled Tomato and Mozzarella Salad
Cut the tomatoes into thick slices, season with salt and pepper, and then brush with a light coating of olive oil. Grill quickly to get nice charred marks, then remove and arrange on a plate. Cut the mozzarella into thick slices and place one slice on each tomato. Use a blowtorch to toast the top of the cheese until light golden brown, then season again with salt and pepper.

Place one spoonful of pesto on top of the cheese and then drizzle the plate with a few drops of olive oil and aged balsamic vinegar. Garnish with basil or cilantro leaves.

---

★ **TIP:** Use the best extra virgin olive oil and aged balsamic vinegar that you can afford for this dish. The flavors will really make a difference.

# GULF SHRIMP AND CRAB-STUFFED AVOCADO

This dish combines my favorite ingredients in a simple and honest way. Shrimp and crab come alive when seasoned simply and left to show their own natural flavors, and it's hard for me to think of a dish that doesn't improve when ripe avocado surrounds it. **Serves 4**

8 ounces baby shrimp, cooked

2 tablespoons mayonnaise

Juice of 1 lemon

½ teaspoon Bonnell's Creole Seasoning Blend (page 182), reserve a pinch for final garnish

1 dash Crystal Hot Sauce

3 tablespoons diced red bell pepper

2 tablespoons chopped fresh chives, reserve a pinch for final garnish

3 tablespoons diced cucumber

1 pinch dry mustard powder

8 ounces jumbo lump fresh blue crabmeat

3 large ripe avocados

In a mixing bowl, combine all ingredients except for the crabmeat and avocado, and mix well. Taste for seasonings and spice level. Adjust with extra hot sauce or a pinch more salt. Pick through the crabmeat carefully to remove any excess shell pieces, but do not break up the large lump pieces. Fold the crabmeat into the mixture at the last minute. Cut the avocados in half and remove the seed. Scoop the avocados out of their skins with a large kitchen spoon and then slice them into thin strips. Place a ring mold (or simply a piece of 6-inch PVC pipe in the center of a plate. Line the inside of the ring with overlapping slices of avocado. Spoon a large portion of the shrimp and crab salad into the middle, then carefully remove the ring by lifting it straight up. Garnish the plate with a sprinkle of seasoning blend and chopped chives, and serve.

# LOBSTER AND CANTALOUPE SALAD WITH TRUFFLE DRESSING

When Texas cantaloupes are in season, there is nothing like the sweet and rich flavor of these beauties. I created this dish for a chef competition that just happened to fall right in the middle of cantaloupe season. I couldn't think of anything better than local cantaloupe, fresh lobster, and a hint of white truffle just to put everything over the top. It just so happened that the judges agreed. **Serves 4 very large portions or 12 appetizers**

---

**Dressing**
1 teaspoon kosher salt
Juice of 1 lemon
1½ tablespoons chopped fresh dill
2 pinches ground black pepper
½ cup mayonnaise
1½ tablespoons white truffle oil
   (optional)

**Salad**
Meat from 2 large lobsters
   (approximately 2 pounds live
   weight each)
1 jalapeño, seeded, and diced
¼ cup peeled, seeded, and diced
   cucumber
7 leaves Belgian endive, chopped
¼ cup finely diced radish
2 tablespoons chopped chives
1 avocado, diced
⅓ cup diced star fruit (optional, but
   makes a great garnish!)
2 large ripe cantaloupes, halved
   and seeded

**Truffle Dressing**
Combine the salt, lemon juice, dill, and pepper. Whisk in the mayonnaise, then drizzle in the truffle oil while continuing to whisk. Fold into the lobster salad mixture and serve immediately. If you plan on serving the salad the next day, dress the lobster salad just prior to serving.

**Lobster and Cantaloupe Salad**
Steam (12 to 14 minutes) or boil (10 to 12 minutes) the lobsters until done, then chill in ice water. Remove the meat from the tail, claws, and knuckles, and chop into large chunks. Remove the meat from the little legs by using a rolling pin. Just pull the legs off and firmly roll from the little claw end; the meat pushes right out of the shell. Combine all chilled lobster meat with the remaining ingredients except for the cantaloupe. Mix the lobster salad well and toss with Truffle Dressing. Use the cantaloupe halves as bowls for the lobster salad and garnish with some fresh herbs, star fruit, or lobster claws. To get the cantaloupe halves to stand up at a slight angle on the plate, cut a small flat spot on the outside of the rind to make them stay in place. For an appetizer portion, cut the cantaloupe halves in half again, then once more to form little triangles. Use a small ice cream scoop or large spoon to create a little pocket right in the middle that can be filled with a smaller amount of lobster salad.

---

★ **TIPS:** Different truffle oils have different strengths. Taste the recipe and decide if more truffle oil is needed in the dressing, or just drizzle a few drops over each portion instead of mixing in the dressing. If you don't want to cook and clean whole lobsters, buy cleaned meat or just tail meat (approximately 1½ to 1 ⅔ pounds total cleaned meat). This dish also works well with shrimp, but I prefer the lobster whenever I can afford it.

# ROASTED TOMATO AND JALAPEÑO SOUP

The heat level in this soup will completely depend on the jalapeños. At some times of the year, the jalapeños can be 3–4 times hotter than at others. If you want to tame down the heat level, remove all seeds and white membranes from the jalapeños before grilling them, or simply use milder peppers. **Serves 4 to 6** (*photo on page 43*)

---

3–4 fresh jalapeños

15 ripe Roma tomatoes

1 extra large sweet onion, sliced into large rings

3–4 cloves garlic, chopped

1½ tablespoons extra virgin olive oil

1½ cups water

Juice of 2 limes

1¼ teaspoon kosher salt

½ teaspoon Bonnell's Creole Seasoning Blend (page 182)

Pepper

2–3 tablespoons sour cream, for garnish

Slice the jalapeños in half, cut off the stems, and remove half of the white veins and seeds. Grill the jalapeños, tomatoes, and onion until well charred on the outsides. In a large soup pot, lightly simmer the onions, tomatoes, jalapeños, and garlic with olive oil and water for 1 to 2 hours. Purée with a stick blender, strain, add lime juice, and season with salt, seasoning, and pepper.

---

★ **OPTIONAL:** Garnish the top with a little lime-flavored sour cream and chopped cilantro or jalapeño slices.

# ROASTED RED PEPPER AND GRILLED CORN CHOWDER

This is a rich and hearty soup that needs special attention right when it's finished. The flavors need to be balanced right at the end to bring out all that this soup has to offer. If the taste seems a touch bitter, add more fresh lime juice and salt to balance it out. With enough seasoning and acidity, this soup just dances on the palate with richness and roasted flavor. **Serves 4**

---

**3 large red bell peppers**
**2 ears fresh corn**
**1 large sweet onion, chopped**
**3–4 cloves garlic, minced**
**1 tablespoon butter**
**1¹/₂ teaspoons kosher salt**
**¹/₄ teaspoon white pepper**
**¹/₂ cup dry white wine**
**1¹/₂ cups heavy cream**
**Juice of 1 lime**
**Cayenne pepper, to taste (optional)**

Roast the red peppers over a grill or stove burner until black on all sides. Place in a plastic bag and let them sweat for 15 to 20 minutes. Using the back of a knife, scrape the skins off the peppers and remove the seeds and stem. Grill corn until lightly browned on all sides, then remove kernels from the cob with a chef's knife. In a large soup pot, sauté onion, garlic, and roasted peppers in butter. When the vegetables are soft, season with salt and pepper. Add the wine and reduce until almost dry; add the cream. Simmer for 5 minutes and then purée with a stick blender until smooth. Add the grilled corn, lime juice, and cayenne and taste for seasonings.

---

# CHILI-RUBBED SMOKED ANTELOPE SALAD WITH CRISPY TOBACCO ONION RINGS

Chef McOwen and I first created this dish to serve to a group of ranch owners who happen to have the largest herd of nilgai antelope in the world on their property. It may sound strange to even hear the words "antelope salad," but this dish is packed with intense flavor. The South Texas antelope from Broken Arrow Ranch is some of the finest meat in the world. It's a rare treat that everyone should try at least once. The presentation alone on this dish is enough to make a true hero out of anyone who can pull this off for a dinner party. Other game meats like venison will work, or a lean cut of beef such as sirloin or tenderloin can be substituted. **Serves 4**

---

1 pound lean antelope top round (our preference is from Broken Arrow Ranch)

2 tablespoons Bonnell's Creole Seasoning Blend (page 182)

1 pound mixed baby lettuces

2 tablespoons Jalapeño Garlic Vinaigrette (see below)

1 ripe avocado

8 ounces Crispy Tobacco Onion Rings (page 172)

½ cup grated queso fresco

8 small organic tomatoes, cut in halves

**Vinaigrette**

4 jalapeño peppers, seeds and veins removed

4 cloves garlic, peeled

3 limes, juice only

2 tablespoons grated Parmesan cheese

1 ½ tablespoons Dijon mustard

1 small bunch cilantro

1 teaspoon kosher salt

½ teaspoon freshly cracked pepper

⅓ cup extra virgin olive oil

⅓ cup vegetable oil

Clean the meat of all silverskin, fat, and connective tissue. Rub with the seasoning on all sides and let stand for at least 2 hours. Using a sweet wood like pecan, smoke slowly at 150 degrees F until an internal temperature of 125 to 130 degrees F is reached. Do not overcook or the meat will become extremely dry. Remove and tightly wrap with plastic. Refrigerate until well chilled. Remove from plastic wrap after is it chilled and slice thinly with a sharp knife, cutting straight across the grain of the meat.

Mix the baby lettuce with the vinaigrette. Place a ring mold (or a large round-shaped cookie cutter) in the center of a plate. Line the inside of the mold with thinly sliced strips of the antelope meat. Add dressed salad greens in the middle and top with slices of avocado and Crispy Tobacco Onion Rings. Sprinkle with queso fresco and garnish the plate with tomatoes.

**Jalapeño Garlic Vinaigrette**

Place all ingredients except oil in a food processor or blender. Mix until uniform texture is reached. Drizzle the oil in last, very slowly. Check salt and pepper seasonings.

---

# VODKA GAZPACHO

On a hot Texas summer day, nothing hits the spot like cold refreshing soup. But just because it's cold, don't think this soup is lacking in richness. When the summer reaches its hottest point, tomatoes and cucumbers (at least in Texas) are simply perfect. This soup is not only refreshing, but it is also one of the healthiest meals. Toasted breadcrumbs or croutons are the perfect texture to complement crisp vegetables. Serve this soup with a spoonful of breadcrumbs in the bottom of the bowl and just a whisper of the frozen vodka floating on top to perk up and carry all of the crisp vegetable flavors. **Serves 2 to 3 bowls or 6 to 8 cups**

6 Roma tomatoes, seeded
1½ large cucumbers, peeled and
    seeded
½ green bell pepper
½ red bell pepper
1 small shallot
3 cloves garlic
Juice of 2 limes
Juice of 1½ oranges
½ bunch fresh basil, leaves only
¼ cup red wine vinegar
¼ cup plus 1 tablespoons extra
    virgin olive oil
2 pinches cayenne pepper
4 teaspoons kosher salt
3 tablespoons toasted panko
    breadcrumbs or croutons, for
    garnish
1 teaspoon per serving vodka,
    for garnish (premium brand
    recommended; keep in freezer)

Run tomatoes, cucumber, bell peppers, shallot, and garlic through a grinder with the smallest plate attached. Combine remaining ingredients, except panko and vodka, and whisk well. Allow to sit refrigerated for 1 hour before serving. The shallots and garlic will have very strong flavors at first but will mellow over time. Serve cold with a topping of toasted breadcrumbs or croutons for a little crunch and drizzle a touch of vodka straight from the freezer on top right before serving.

# WHITE GAZPACHO

One of the most fun things about this soup is the surprise on diners' faces when they assume that since it's white, it must be bland. The tomatoes, cucumbers, and peppers carry most of the load in this dish, but it's the few drops of white truffle oil that bring it all together. I often serve this as a shooter for cocktail parties with just a few eggs of caviar floating right on top. **Serves 2 to 3 bowls or 6 to 8 cups**

---

3 large yellow tomatoes
2 yellow bell peppers, seeded
2 large cucumbers, peeled and
   seeded
½ small sweet onion
6 celery ribs (the lighter in color,
   the better; no leaves)
1 ⅔ cups heavy cream or half-and-
   half
4 tablespoons extra virgin olive oil
Juice of 4 limes
1¼ teaspoons salt
½ teaspoon white pepper
White winter truffle oil, for garnish
   (2–3 drops per serving)
Chopped fresh chives or chive
   blossoms, for garnish
Caviar, for garnish (optional)

Run tomatoes, bell peppers, cucumbers, onion, and celery through a grinder with the small plate attached. Combine with cream, oil, and lime juice, season with salt and pepper, and whisk thoroughly to combine. Allow to sit in the refrigerator for at least 1 hour. Serve chilled with a few drops of white winter truffle oil on top and a few chopped chives. For the ultimate indulgence, add a small amount of fine caviar on top and serve with chilled champagne!

---

# WILD MUSHROOM AND DUCK GUMBO

Everything I thought about gumbo was revolutionized the instant I tasted gumbo in the French Quarter of New Orleans. After working at Mr. B's as part of a culinary externship, I began working on my own version of "real" gumbo. This version is as rich as any soup you can possibly imagine. It's perfect for a cold winter day when the wild mushrooms are in season (and so are the ducks for that matter), and a hot steamy bowl of gumbo is needed to warm up the soul. **Serves 8 to 10 bowls**

---

**Duck Confit**

4 fresh duck legs

1 tablespoon kosher salt

2 teaspoons Bonnell's Creole Seasoning Blend (page 182)

1 cup canola oil

**Gumbo**

1/2 pound button mushrooms

1/2 pound shiitake mushrooms

1/2 pound crimini mushrooms

1/2 pound portobello mushrooms

1/2 pound oyster mushrooms

8 tablespoons butter

1/2 cup flour

2 tablespoons canola oil

5 fresh thyme sprigs

1 1/2 Texas 1015 onions or other sweet onions, diced

1 1/2 ribs celery, diced

1 1/2 tablespoons chopped garlic

1 red bell pepper, diced

1 green bell pepper, diced

1 poblano pepper, diced

1/2 cup Bonnell's Creole Seasoning Blend (page 182)

1 teaspoon salt

1/4 teaspoon ground black pepper

1 gallon chicken stock

1/4 cup Frank's RedHot Sauce

1/4 cup Worcestershire sauce

1 1/2 pounds frozen okra, chopped

**Duck Confit**

On the day before cooking the duck, rub the duck legs thoroughly with salt and seasoning and allow to marinate for 24 hours. On the following day, place the legs in a 250-degree F pecan wood smoker for 1 hour. Remove the legs from the smoker and place in a Dutch-oven–type roasting pan with a tight-fitting lid and add the canola oil. Cook covered on the stovetop on low or in the oven at 250 degrees F for 2 to 3 hours, or until the legs become tender. Remove the meat from the bone and shred by hand when cool enough to handle. Discard the fat, skin, and oil. Keep the meat refrigerated until ready to use.

**Gumbo**

Clean and chop all the mushrooms. Cook the butter and flour together in a heavy-bottom pan to form a roux. Keep stirring continuously over medium heat until the roux has reached a dark caramel color. Remove from the heat and set aside.

In a separate large sauté pan, sauté mushrooms in canola oil with thyme sprigs until soft. In a separate large soup pot, sauté onions, celery, garlic, and peppers. Once the onion has softened, add seasonings, stock, hot sauce, and Worcestershire sauce, and bring to a simmer. Whisk in the cooled roux vigorously, then add the mushrooms and okra to the mix; remove the thyme stems. Allow all ingredients to simmer together for at least 5 minutes. Ladle the hot gumbo into bowls and top each serving with warm duck confit and cooked white rice (optional).

---

# WILTED SPINACH SALAD WITH BLUE CRAB, CHILIED PECANS, AND WARM BACON VINAIGRETTE

A perfectly executed spinach salad is truly a thing of beauty. When spinach is raw, it's too squeaky on the teeth, but when it's tossed with a warm bacon vinaigrette to just slightly wilt the greens, it's nothing short of perfection on a plate. Adding crabmeat and spiced pecans is just a bonus that puts this salad in a league of its own. **Serves 6**

---

### Vinaigrette
3 ounces slab bacon, diced
1 small Spanish onion, chopped
1 large clove garlic, minced
1/4 cup sherry vinegar
2 tablespoons cream sherry
1/4 cup dry white wine
3/4 cup extra virgin olive oil
1 teaspoon Dijon mustard
1/2 teaspoon Worcestershire sauce
3/4 teaspoon kosher salt

### Pecans
1/2 cup pecan halves
1 1/2 teaspoons olive oil
1 teaspoon Bonnell's Creole
    Seasoning Blend (page 182)
1/2 teaspoon chili powder

### Salad
1–1 1/2 pounds cleaned fresh
    baby spinach
1 pound jumbo lump crabmeat,
    picked through for shell pieces

### Warm Bacon Vinaigrette
In a medium saucepan, render the bacon slowly until slightly browned. Remove and set aside. In the same pan, caramelize the onion in the bacon drippings (add a touch of oil if the pan gets dry). When the onion has browned, add the garlic, then deglaze with vinegar and wine, and let reduce (be careful, it may flame) by more than half. Add the remaining ingredients, including the bacon, and check for seasonings. If using immediately, keep warm.

### Chilied Pecans
Toss all ingredients in a mixing bowl until well combined. Bake coated pecans at 350 degrees F until toasted, about 5 to 7 minutes.

### Wilted Spinach Salad
Place spinach and the chilied pecans in a large salad bowl. Add about 2 to 3 tablespoons warm dressing and toss slightly just to wilt the spinach. Place the spinach mixture on a platter or individual plates. Add the crabmeat and a little more dressing to the same bowl and toss to coat. Be careful not to break up the beautiful large crab pieces. Top each salad or the platter with the dressed crabmeat and serve immediately. This salad must be tossed right at the last minute.

---

★ **NOTE:** This dressing can be made ahead of time and kept in the refrigerator. It will probably solidify, but it can be warmed up just prior to serving. Do not serve as a cold salad dressing.

# LEMON CAESAR SALAD WITH SOUTHWESTERN CROUTONS

A classic Caesar salad is hard to beat and has stood the test of time. I like to use lemon for the acidic component and I add just a touch of spice to the croutons. **Serves 4 to 6**

---

**Dressing**
1 egg yolk
1 anchovy fillet (optional)
Juice of 2 lemons (reserve peel for zesting)
1 teaspoon Worcestershire Sauce
1 teaspoon Dijon mustard
1 dash hot sauce
1 small clove garlic
1 tablespoon freshly grated Parmesan cheese
1/8 teaspoon salt
1 pinch ground white pepper
5 tablespoons extra virgin olive oil

**Croutons**
1 baguette
1 cup butter
1/2 bunch fresh flat-leaf parsley, chopped
1 tablespoon chopped garlic
2 tablespoons Bonnell's Creole Seasoning Blend (page 182)

**Salad**
2 hearts of romaine lettuce
4 tablespoons freshly grated Parmesan cheese
Zest of 1 lemon

**Lemon Caesar Dressing**
In a food processor, combine all ingredients except the olive oil. Purée until a smooth consistency is reached. It may be necessary to stop the blades and scrape down the sides of the bowl a few times with a rubber spatula. While the mixture is puréeing, slowly drizzle in the oil until it reaches a smooth creamy texture; set aside.

**Southwestern Croutons**
Cut the baguette into large cubes for croutons. Melt the butter and combine with parsley, garlic, and seasoning; pour mixture over the bread. Toss in a large mixing bowl to coat the bread cubes evenly and then toast them on a baking sheet in a 350-degree F oven for approximately 10 minutes, or until lightly crisp and golden brown.

**Caesar Salad**
Chop the lettuce into bite-size ribbons, dress well with Caesar dressing, and toss with desired amount of grated Parmesan cheese and Southwestern Croutons. For a little added flavor, garnish with a touch of freshly grated lemon zest just before serving. The Parmesan and lemon zest can be grated tableside for flair in presentation.

---

# SEAFOOD AND SHELLFISH

★ Barbequed Oysters with Anaheim Chile–Lime Sauce ★
★ Crispy Flounder with Shaved Fennel Slaw ★
★ Grilled Arctic Char with Jumbo Lump Crab and Cascabel Chile Sauce ★
★ Grilled Trout with Mango Pico de Gallo ★
★ Jumbo Lump Crab Cakes with Scallion-Lime Aioli ★
★ Grilled Lobster and Scallions with Herb-Infused Olive Oil ★
★ Pecan-Crusted Texas Redfish with Baby Shrimp, Tomato, and Cilantro Butter Sauce ★
★ Seared Texas Shrimp and Tomatoes with Guajillo Chile Sauce ★
★ Shrimp and Redfish Ceviche ★
★ Pumpkin Seed–Crusted Striped Bass ★
★ Diver Scallops with Painted Pony Bean Purée ★

Texans are lucky to have such a bountiful gulf coastline that readily produces incredibly diverse seafood. Jet travel allows us to bring in fresh seafood from all corners of the globe these days, but there's still nothing quite like fresh seafood that comes in still dripping with briny seawater. I feel sorry for anyone who hasn't shucked a live oyster and experienced the salty explosion that you can only get when the actual seawater is still there to enhance the crisp texture of a really fresh oyster. We Texans have a vast array of great seafood options at our disposal, and we tend to utilize them quite well. Redfish may have been on the decline at one time, but high-quality aqua-farming techniques have brought this species back in enormous numbers and superb quality for us to enjoy year-round. Shrimp never go out of season around here, and fresh-picked blue crabmeat is always easy to find. Although those seafood staples are readily available, generally my favorite thing about seafood is the uncertain nature of what might be available from day to day. I can count on my meat purveyors to have the same list of items

pretty much every day, but calling the fish suppliers is an adventure every single time. It really helps me stay on my toes not knowing what kind of fresh fish I can count on for tomorrow's order. It's always important to get to know your fishmonger and use what's fresh today, not necessarily what is called for in a recipe. Be flexible when it comes to fish, because the freshest is always the best in the fish department.

Fish is one of the easiest kinds of meat to prepare, although most people are either intimidated or just too downright scared to even attempt it. Fish really absorbs outdoor flavors well, so using a wood-burning grill is a great option. Remember to always apply a very thin layer of oil to the fish before it hits the hot grill so it won't stick. I like the high-temp aerosol sprays of 100-percent canola oil for applying an even coat of oil to fish without going overboard. Pan-searing fish works well too, especially in a hot nonstick or cast-iron pan. Always remember to season fish well and never overcook. No matter what kind of preparation you use for fish, it's going to be dry if it's overcooked. ★

*Shrimp and Redfish Ceviche, recipe on page 86.*

# BARBEQUED OYSTERS WITH ANAHEIM CHILE-LIME SAUCE

This is one of my favorite appetizers to serve outside around the grill. Enlist one of your friends to help shuck the oysters while you grill them. **Serves 6 to 8**

---

**Sauce**
1 sweet onion, diced
3 cloves garlic, minced
1 tablespoon olive oil
¼ cup white wine
1½ cups chicken stock
1 (14-ounce) can chopped tomatoes
6 dried Anaheim chiles, seeded and
    stemmed
1½ teaspoons kosher salt
1 pinch ground black pepper
Juice of 2 limes

**Oysters**
2 dozen live oysters in the shells

**Anaheim Chile-Lime Sauce**
Sauté onion and garlic in the olive oil until soft. Deglaze with wine and reduce liquid until the pan is almost dry. Add remaining ingredients, except for the lime juice, and simmer for 8 to 10 minutes, or until chiles have completely softened and hydrated. Purée well with a stick blender and add lime juice. This sauce can be used as is, or it can be strained if it's a little chunky.

**Barbecued Oysters**
Shuck the oysters and discard the top shell. Be sure to slightly cut the muscle that attaches the oyster to the bottom shell, as if you were serving them raw. Lay the oysters, shell down, right on top of a hot wood-burning grill and then top each one with a generous spoonful of the chile-lime sauce. Cook until the sauce begins to bubble in the shells. Remove carefully with tongs and serve. The oysters will cook as they simmer in the sauce.

---

# CRISPY FLOUNDER WITH SHAVED FENNEL SLAW

Flounder is a delicately flavored fish from the Gulf that most sportsmen are more than familiar with. The flesh is moist and flaky, and I love putting a little texture like crispy panko breadcrumbs on the outside to give a little crunch to this mild fish. **Serves 4 large portions**

---

**Slaw**

6 ounces fennel bulb

5 ounces fresh sunchokes (substitute radish if sunchokes are out of season)

1 serrano pepper

4 ounces hearts of palm

Fennel fronds, chopped

Juice of 1 lime

2–4 tablespoons mayonnaise

1/4 teaspoon salt

1/8 teaspoon freshly ground black pepper

**Crispy Flounder**

4 boneless and skinless flounder fillets

Salt and pepper, to taste

1/2 cup flour

2 eggs

1/4 cup milk

1/2 cup panko breadcrumbs

1/2 teaspoon salt

1/3 teaspoon cracked black pepper

Olive oil, enough to just barely cover the bottom of a nonstick sauté pan

4–6 baby artichokes, cooked and quartered

1 Roma tomato, seeded and diced

2 tablespoons chopped scallions

1 clove garlic, minced

1 lemon, thinly sliced

4 tablespoons butter

**Shaved Fennel Slaw**

Remove the hard core of the fennel bulb and then use a mandolin or a very sharp knife to shave the fennel as thinly as possible. Wash the sunchokes under cold water, scrub to remove any dirt, but do not peel. Using the mandolin again, julienne the sunchokes into very thin long strips. This machine will save you tremendous amounts of time for this recipe. Shave the serrano very thin. If you want to cut down on the heat, remove the seeds and veins of the serrano, or leave out completely. Cut the hearts of palm into half moons and then add a few fennel fronds (the thin green tops that look like dill). Add all of the ingredients together in a mixing bowl and adjust the salt and pepper if necessary.

**Crispy Flounder**

Season the fish lightly with salt and pepper, then follow the standard breading procedure of dredging in flour, then dipping in eggwash (egg and milk combined), then dredging in breadcrumbs mixed with salt and pepper to coat completely on all sides. In a hot sauté pan, brown the fish on both sides in a little olive oil. If the fillets are thin, this will be enough cooking. If they are thicker pieces, they can be finished in a 375-degree F oven until done. Cook the fish in batches of 1 to 2 fillets per batch to avoid overcrowding the pan. Drain the flounder on paper towels after cooking. If the pan gets dry while cooking, add a touch more olive oil. After the fish is cooked, quickly sauté the artichokes, tomatoes, scallions, and garlic in the same pan you used for the fish. After about 1 minute, turn the heat to low, add the lemon slices and butter, and swirl the pan until the butter is completely melted. Swirl continuously while the butter is melting to get a nice emulsified rich sauce. Season lightly with a pinch of salt and pepper just before serving. Plate the fillets over a mound of fennel and sunchoke slaw, pour the hot buttery sauce right over the top, and serve immediately.

---

# GRILLED ARCTIC CHAR WITH JUMBO LUMP CRAB AND CASCABEL CHILE SAUCE

Arctic char is a freshwater fish in the salmon family with an extremely mild and delicate salmon flavor. I love pairing this particular fish with a rustic chile like the cascabel. It adds an earthy flavor to fish with just enough spice to keep it interesting, but not enough to hurt anybody. **Serves 4**

Sauce
1 small sweet onion, diced
2 large cloves garlic, minced
1 tablespoon olive oil
7–8 cascabel chiles, seeded and
    stemmed
¼ cup dry white wine
1½ cups chicken stock
1 (12-ounce) can chopped tomatoes
¼ teaspoon kosher salt
Juice of 2 limes

Char with Crab
4 (6–8 ounce) boneless and skinless
    Arctic char fillets
1 teaspoon kosher salt,
    plus more to taste
½ teaspoon freshly ground
    black pepper
2 tablespoons canola oil (for grilling)
2 small cloves garlic, minced
6 tablespoons butter, divided
1 pound jumbo lump crabmeat
⅓ cup Cascabel Chile Sauce
Juice of ½ lime

### Cascabel Chile Sauce

In a small saucepan, lightly sauté the onion and garlic in olive oil until soft, then add the cascabels. Deglaze the pan with wine and reduce liquid until the pan is almost dry. Add remaining ingredients, except for the lime juice, and simmer for 8 to 10 minutes, or until the cascabels have softened and rehydrated. Purée the mixture with a stick blender until smooth, and strain. Squeeze in fresh lime juice and cool.

### Grilled Arctic Char with Jumbo Lump Crab

Lay the fish fillets on a cutting board and pat dry with paper towels. Season well with salt and pepper on both sides, then lightly brush an even coating of canola oil on each side as well. Grill over mesquite wood on both sides until done, then set on dinner plates and keep warm while making the sauce. In a large sauté pan, quickly cook the garlic in 1 teaspoon butter, but do not allow it to brown. Add the crab pieces and toss just to coat. Add the chile sauce to the pan and bring to a simmer. As the sauce simmers, add the rest of the butter and the lime juice, and season with just a pinch of salt. Swirl the pan to incorporate the butter, as it melts, pour the entire contents evenly over each fillet.

# GRILLED TROUT WITH MANGO PICO DE GALLO

Rainbow trout are a shining example of what can happen when the right kind of aquaculture techniques are utilized in an eco-friendly way. Anyone in the United States can get fresh trout fillets on any day of the year, while wild trout populations still thrive and flourish. Grilling this fish brings some bold flavor to an otherwise mild species that pairs perfectly with a sweet, tangy, slightly spicy mango pico. **Serves 2**

---

### Pico de Gallo
1 small ripe mango, peeled and finely diced
3 Roma tomatoes, seeded and finely diced
½ purple onion, finely diced
2 jalapeño peppers, seeded, deveined (leave seeds in if you like it hot!), and diced
2 heaping tablespoons chopped cilantro
Juice of 2 limes
½ teaspoon kosher salt
1 pinch ground black pepper

### Trout
2 (8–10 ounce) farm-raised rainbow trout fillets, butterflied and deboned, skin on
1 tablespoon Bonnell's Creole Seasoning Blend (page 182)
Canola oil for grilling

### Mango Pico de Gallo
Combine all ingredients in a mixing bowl and mix well. Serve immediately. If you plan to use the following day, omit the lime juice, salt, and pepper until ready to serve, or the mixture will become soupy as the juices are drawn out from each ingredient. It is very important to use quickly once the acidic lime juice and salt have been added.

### Grilled Trout
Be sure the trout fillets are cleaned well and then patted dry with a paper towel. Dust liberally with the seasoning on the flesh side, then lightly brush with canola oil. Grill over a very hot woodburning grill for 1½ to 2 minutes per side just until done, remove, top with Mango Pico de Gallo, and serve. I like to use pecan wood or mesquite wood for really flavorful fish. While the fish is grilling on one side, lightly brush the top with oil just before flipping to keep the skin from sticking to the grill.

---

★ **NOTE:** If you have trouble with fish sticking to the grill, use a nonstick fish-grilling basket and place over the grill in the hottest part. This doesn't impart quite as much flavor as actual contact with the hot grill bars, but it's foolproof for keeping fish together in one piece.

# JUMBO LUMP CRAB CAKES WITH SCALLION-LIME AIOLI

There is just no acceptable substitute for real crabmeat in Texas. When I talk about crab, I always mean the real stuff—the expensive stuff. For me, any crab cake that's more cake than crab isn't worth eating. I want my crab cakes to be filled with huge chunks of jumbo lump crab with crab claw meat for a binder, lightly coated on the outside with breadcrumbs just to give some texture, but never used as a filler. Everyone has tried a crab cake somewhere, but few people have had a really good one. This recipe is sure to impress even the most skeptical of crab lovers. **Yields 12 to 15 cakes**

---

### Aioli
2 egg yolks
2 tablespoons Dijon mustard
1/2 teaspoon cayenne pepper
1 bunch scallions (green parts only),
    chopped
Juice of 3 limes
1/4 teaspoon kosher salt
1–2 dashes hot sauce
2 cups vegetable oil

### Crab Cakes
1 red bell pepper, finely diced
1 bunch scallions
    (green parts only), chopped
2 eggs
3/4 cup mayonnaise
1 tablespoon Dijon mustard
1 tablespoon Worcestershire sauce
1 tablespoon hot sauce (Frank's
    RedHot, Cholula, or Texas
    Champagne are my favorites)
1 teaspoon Bonnell's Creole
    Seasoning Blend (page 182)
1 pound crab claw meat
1 pound jumbo lump crabmeat
2 cups panko breadcrumbs
1/2 teaspoon kosher salt

### Scallion-Lime Aioli
In a food processor or blender, combine all ingredients except for the oil and blend well. Slowly drizzle in the oil while the machine is running to form a smooth mayonnaise consistency.

### Jumbo Lump Crab Cakes
Mix together all ingredients except crab, breadcrumbs, and salt. Gently fold in crab claw meat, then the jumbo lump last, being extremely careful not to break up the big pieces. Form into 3-ounce cakes, about 1/3 cup each. They will be very wet and messy at this point. Place the panko crumbs into a mixing bowl and gently drop in one cake at a time. Coat the outside of each cake with the crumbs by gently pressing with your hands. Do not mix the breadcrumbs into the crab cake mix, and be careful not to press so hard that the juices all squeeze out of the cakes. These cakes will be quite messy to prepare but should be juicy and delicious if prepared properly. Heat a deep fryer filled with canola oil to 350 degrees F and fry the cakes until golden brown and crispy on the outside. The cakes can also be pan-fried to avoid the mess of a deep fryer, but they will need to be pressed somewhat flatter to cook this way. When the cakes are cooked, drain on paper towels and sprinkle immediately with kosher salt. Serve hot with a drizzle of the aioli.

---

# GRILLED LOBSTER AND SCALLIONS WITH HERB-INFUSED OLIVE OIL

The complexity of olive oil that's been infused with grilled herbs really ties this dish together. Use a high-quality extra virgin olive oil for this dish, since the oil won't actually be cooked. This is a great way to serve lobster with tremendous flavor but without drowning it in butter. The grilled scallions take on a very sweet, toasted flavor when grilled. I love cooking this dish when people are crowded around the grill. It's a simple technique that people love to watch and anyone can master. **Serves 4**

**2–3 fresh sprigs each: thyme, rosemary, oregano, and dill**
**1 cup extra virgin olive oil**
**2 (10–12 ounce each) lobster tails**
**Pinch of kosher salt and ground black pepper**
**2 bunches fresh scallions**

Tie the sprigs of fresh herbs together with butcher's twine to form a small brush. Dip the end of the brush into the olive oil and allow to soak while preparing the other items. Prepare the lobster tails by cutting them in half lengthwise and removing any veins; then season lightly with salt and pepper. Burn a mesquite wood fire down to bright red-hot coals. Use the herb brush to brush an area of the grill bars right over the coals with oil and place a lobster tail, meat side down, in that spot. This will prevent the lobster from sticking to the grill. Return the brush to the oil and brush another spot on the grill, until each of the tails has been placed face down. Each time the herbs brush the hot grill, they will get a slightly more intense grilled flavor. Keep placing the herbs back into the bowl of olive oil between each brushing, which will intensify the flavor of the oil. Grill the tails on the first side for 1 to 2 minutes, then turn them over and cook until they simmer inside their shells. Using the herb brush, grill the scallions in the same manner until they wilt and lightly darken on each side. Season them lightly with salt and pepper while grilling, then arrange them on a large platter. Remove the tails from the grill when they are ready, then remove the meat from the shells (if desired). Place the tails on top of the scallions, drizzle the platter liberally with the herb-infused oil, and serve.

# PECAN-CRUSTED TEXAS REDFISH WITH BABY SHRIMP, TOMATO, AND CILANTRO BUTTER SAUCE

Redfish is a true Texas treasure. It's been popular with sportsmen for quite some time, but in recent years several very reputable aquafarms have begun to produce these fish near the Texas gulf coast. The slightly firm texture, sweet and tender meat, and year-round availability make this fish one that I consistently serve all year long. I love adding just a little texture and complexity by coating one side with pecans. Texas striped bass, grouper, or red snapper all have a nice flaky and delicate flavor that work very well for this recipe. **Serves 2**

---

4 tablespoons Bonnell's Creole
    Seasoning Blend (page 182)
½ cup fresh pecan halves
2 (8-ounce) boneless and skinless
    fresh Redfish fillets
1 tablespoon olive oil (approximately,
    depending on your pan size)
7–10 baby shrimp
1 small shallot, minced
½ clove garlic, minced
¼–⅓ cup dry white wine
2 tablespoons chopped tomato
1 teaspoon chopped cilantro
3 tablespoons butter
¼ teaspoon kosher salt
Pepper, to taste
Juice of ½ lime

Mix the seasoning with the pecan halves and pulse in a food processor several times until the nuts only have a few large pieces left; scatter the mix over a large plate. Lay the clean and dry fish fillets down on top of the seasonings and press lightly so the nuts will stick. (Be sure to lay the pretty side—or what we in the industry call the presentation side—down in the nuts. They will end up facing up on the finished plate.) In a large sauté pan, drizzle a little olive oil in and then gently place the fish fillets pecan-side-down. Gently shake the pan back and forth to keep the fish from sticking to the bottom of the pan. Nonstick pans work exceptionally well for cooking fish. Cook on the first side for approximately 1½ to 2 minutes, being careful not to let the nuts burn. (If the pecans turn black and smoke, the dish must be started over, using a cooler pan.) Turn the fillets over gently and then continue cooking until the fish is done. If the fish is very thick, place the entire pan into a 375-degree F oven (as long as it's an oven-safe pan) to finish cooking. Remove fillets from the pan and let rest on a warm plate while you make the sauce. Add shrimp, shallot, and garlic to the same fish pan, turn up the heat to high, and sauté lightly. Add the wine and reduce the liquid by a little more than half; add the tomatoes, cilantro, and butter. Swirl the entire contents continually until the butter melts, season lightly with salt and pepper, squeeze in the lime juice, spoon sauce over the fillets, and serve immediately.

---

# SEARED TEXAS SHRIMP AND TOMATOES WITH GUAJILLO CHILE SAUCE

Guajillo chiles have the perfect amount of rustic earthy flavor and gentle heat that pairs perfectly with grilled seafood. I love the bright deep-red color that comes out when these chiles are rehydrated and the dramatic presentation that this kind of sauce can create. **Serves 4**

---

### Sauce
1 small onion, diced
3 cloves garlic, minced
1½ teaspoons olive oil
6 dried guajillo chiles, seeded
   and stemmed
¼ cup white wine
1½ cups chicken stock
1 (12-ounce) can chopped tomatoes
1½ teaspoons kosher salt
Juice of 1 lime

### Shrimp and Tomatoes
12 large (16–20 count)
   wild Texas white shrimp
1 teaspoon salt
½ teaspoon cracked black pepper
2 large red beefsteak tomatoes
2 large yellow beefsteak tomatoes
1 tablespoon olive oil

### Guajillo Chile Sauce
Sauté the onion and garlic in olive oil until the onion begins to soften; add the guajillo chiles. Deglaze the pan with a splash of wine and reduce liquid until the pan is almost dry. Add remaining ingredients except the lime juice and bring to a simmer. Allow to simmer on low heat for 8-10 minutes, stirring occasionally. Once the guajillos have rehydrated, purée the mixture with a stick blender until smooth. Add the lime juice just before serving. If this sauce has a few pieces of guajillo that won't break down, strain them out to make the sauce nice and smooth for presentation, or it can be left more rustic as is. Just before serving, taste the sauce for seasonings. If it seems bland or slightly bitter, adjust with more lime and salt to balance it out.

### Grilled Shrimp and Tomatoes
Peel the shrimp, remove the heads, and devein by cutting a thin slice down the back line and remove any black or brown matter. Season lightly with salt and pepper, then sear very quickly in a hot nonstick or cast-iron pan until done. This should take no longer than 1 to 2 minutes. Slice the tomatoes into thick round steaks and lightly drizzle with olive oil. Season lightly with salt and pepper on both sides and grill on high heat for 1 minute on each side. Arrange the plate with alternating yellow and red grilled tomato slices stacked in the center of a plate; arrange 3 seared shrimp on the top. Pour guajillo chile sauce around the plate or over the top of the stack, and serve.

---

# SHRIMP AND REDFISH CEVICHE

Ceviche is incredibly popular in Texas these days, and for good reason. It should go without saying, but only the very freshest seafood is appropriate for this recipe. This dish can be served informally like a dip with fresh tortilla chips or fancied up in a martini glass for an upscale presentation. The textures and flavors are crisp and acidic, and pair very nicely with Sauvignon Blanc. **Serves 6 appetizer portions** *(photo on page 69)*

---

1 (8-ounce) boneless, skinless redfish fillet

1 pound baby shrimp

Juice of 8 limes

1 large cucumber, peeled, seeded, and diced

1 jalapeño, diced (seeds optional)

½ bunch scallions (green parts only), chopped

5 Roma tomatoes, peeled, seeded and chopped

½ bunch cilantro, chopped

1 cup Bloody Mary mix

4 ripe avocados, diced

½ teaspoon kosher salt

Cut the redfish into pieces roughly the same size as the baby shrimp. Place the redfish and baby shrimp into a colander and rinse thoroughly under cold water. Place them in a plastic container, cover completely with fresh lime juice, and allow them to sit in the refrigerator overnight. The acid in the lime juice will "cook" the seafood. The following day, remove the seafood from the fridge and strain off the lime juice. Mix the seafood with all other ingredients and finish with a squeeze of fresh lime juice. Serve with fresh, warm corn tortilla chips for dipping or garnish with thin tortilla strips and avocado slices for a fancier presentation.

---

# PUMPKIN SEED–CRUSTED STRIPED BASS

Striped bass are a great gamefish for sportsmen and have been transplanted to many of the larger lakes in Texas. Striped bass are also available from several aquafarms, but the wild variety will have more flavor and a much firmer texture.
**Serves 1**

2 tablespoons Bonnell's Creole
   Seasoning Blend (page 182)
1/2 cup coarsely chopped pumpkin
   seeds (pepitas)
1 (6–8 ounce) boneless, skinless
   striped bass fillet
2 teaspoons olive oil
1 small shallot, minced
1/2 clove garlic, minced
3 tablespoons white wine
2 tablespoons butter
1 teaspoon chopped fresh dill
Pinch of kosher salt
Juice of 1 lemon

Mix the seasoning with pumpkin seeds (they can be easily chopped in a food processor) and scatter on a large plate. Lay the clean, dry fish fillet on top of the seasonings and press lightly so the seeds will stick. In a hot pan, drizzle the olive oil, then gently place the fish fillet with seeds facing down. Gently shake the pan back and forth to keep the fish from sticking. Nonstick pans work very well for cooking fish. Cook on the first side for approximately 1 1/2 minutes, being careful not to let the nuts burn. (If the nuts turn black, the dish must be started over, using a slightly cooler pan.) Turn the fillet over gently and then continue cooking until the fish is done. (Putting the entire pan into the oven works well for this step, especially if the fillet is very thick.) Remove fillet from the pan and let rest on a warm dinner plate. In the same pan, turn the heat to high and lightly sauté the shallot and garlic. Deglaze the pan with wine and reduce liquid until the pan is almost dry. Add the butter and dill, and swirl until the butter is just barely melted. Season with a pinch of kosher salt and squeeze in the fresh lemon juice. Swirl to incorporate, pour sauce over the fish, and serve.

# DIVER SCALLOPS WITH
# PAINTED PONY BEAN PURÉE

The tender, sweet flavor of scallops really contrasts well with the creamy, rustic taste of this heirloom variety of beans. I love using dried chiles such as pasillas to accent the flavor of beans. **Serves 5 entrées or 15 appetizers**

---

Purée

1 small onion, diced
1 strip bacon, diced
2 cloves garlic
2 tablespoons olive oil
1 pound dried painted pony beans
1 quart chicken stock
1 pasilla chile, stemmed and seeded
Salt and pepper, to taste

Sauce

4 tablespoons butter
4 tablespoons flour
1 yellow onion
1 red bell pepper
1 green bell pepper
1/2 jalapeño
1 small rib celery
1/2 carrot
1 tablespoon minced garlic
3 teaspoons Bonnell's Creole
   Seasoning Blend (page 182)
2 cups diced canned tomatoes
3 cups chicken stock
Salt and pepper, to taste

Scallops

15 large diver scallops, cleaned
15 strips bacon
15 toothpicks
Salt and pepper, to taste
3 teaspoons clarified butter (ghee)

**Painted Pony Bean Purée**

In a large soup pot, sauté the onion, bacon, and garlic in olive oil until soft, then add the remaining ingredients. Be sure there is enough liquid to just cover the beans, season well with salt and pepper, cover, and bring to a simmer. Remove the cover after 30 minutes and simmer another 30 minutes, or until the beans are tender. Purée with a stick blender until smooth. If the purée becomes too thin or watery, reduce liquid to thicken. If the beans become too thick, adjust with a little more stock. Check the seasonings before serving.

**Creole Sauce**

In a large saucepan, melt the butter and add the flour. Stir constantly, cooking the roux until it is caramel colored. Add the onion, peppers, jalapeño, celery, carrot, garlic, and seasoning and cook 2 minutes. Add tomatoes and whisk in chicken stock; simmer lightly for 15 minutes. Purée and season to taste.

**Diver Scallops**

Clean the scallops well, remove the small muscle on the side if it's still attached, and then blot dry with paper towels. Wrap each scallop tightly with a strip of bacon and hold the bacon in place by piercing through the middle with a toothpick. Season the scallops on both sides with salt and pepper, and then sear over very high heat in a teaspoon of clarified butter. Nonstick or well-seasoned cast-iron pans work best for scallops. Only sear 4 to 5 scallops per pan to ensure that the pan does not overcrowd. Be sure to get a good dark caramelized sear on both flat sides of the scallop and then finish cooking in a 400-degree F oven for approximately 5 minutes. The time may vary, depending on the size and thickness of the scallops. When the scallops are done, serve on top of the bean purée with a small spoonful of Creole sauce.

---

# POLLTRY

★ Creole-Smoked Free-Range Chicken ★
★ Duck Meatballs Marinara ★
★ Grilled Texas Quail with Jalapeño Cream Sauce ★
★ Roasted Stuffed Quail with Cornbread and Andouille Sausage ★
★ Mushroom-Stuffed Chukar Partridge with Sage Gravy ★
★ Quail Raviolis ★
★ Seared Duck Breast with Wild Mushroom and Cabernet Demiglace ★
★ Smoked Wild Turkey ★
★ Southwestern Chicken Stack ★
★ Pheasant Stuffed with Goat Cheese and Herbs in Phyllo ★

---

Every type of game bird has a texture and flavor profile that's all its own, and each should be treated with equal respect. Nothing really "tastes just like chicken." Even when it comes to chicken, not all birds are created equally. The difference between birds from Dominion Farms that have been raised naturally and free-roaming differ immensely from the bargain brand at my local grocery store. I was raised on a variety of different game birds, usually the ones that my brother and I managed to knock down with a shotgun each year, and I have always had a special place in my heart for the flavor and unique texture of different wild birds. For the past twenty-six years, I've been responsible for harvesting the Thanksgiving family turkey (quite a bit of pressure, I might add), and when it is served side by side with a store-bought turkey, most family members go back for the wild bird when it's time for seconds. That's not to say that there is anything inherently wrong with domestically raised turkey or chicken, but rather that there is just so much more out there to enjoy. If you can learn to treat each different type of bird as its own unique product, then the possibilities become endless. ★

# CREOLE-SMOKED
# FREE-RANGE CHICKEN

This recipe will work for any type of chicken, but the quality of free-range birds is hard to beat. The birds from Dominion Farms are fed an all-natural diet and they are raised walking through the grass, not stacked in chicken coops. The flavor of natural chicken is much richer and really shows through in this type of preparation. **Serves 2 to 4**

¼ cup Bonnell's Creole Seasoning
   Blend (page 182)
¼ cup brown sugar
1 whole free-range chicken

Combine the seasoning with the brown sugar and rub the chicken completely inside and out with the mixture. Refrigerate and allow to marinate for 1 to 2 hours. Preheat a smoker with pecan wood to 225 degrees F, then place the bird in and allow to smoke until the internal temperature reaches 165 degrees F. The chicken can be served whole or cut into smaller pieces. If using for pulled chicken, remove the bird from the smoker and allow to cool slightly before pulling the meat. Tear the meat into usable portions and mix the light and dark meats together. Be sure to remove any pieces of bone, skin, or cartilage for pulled chicken.

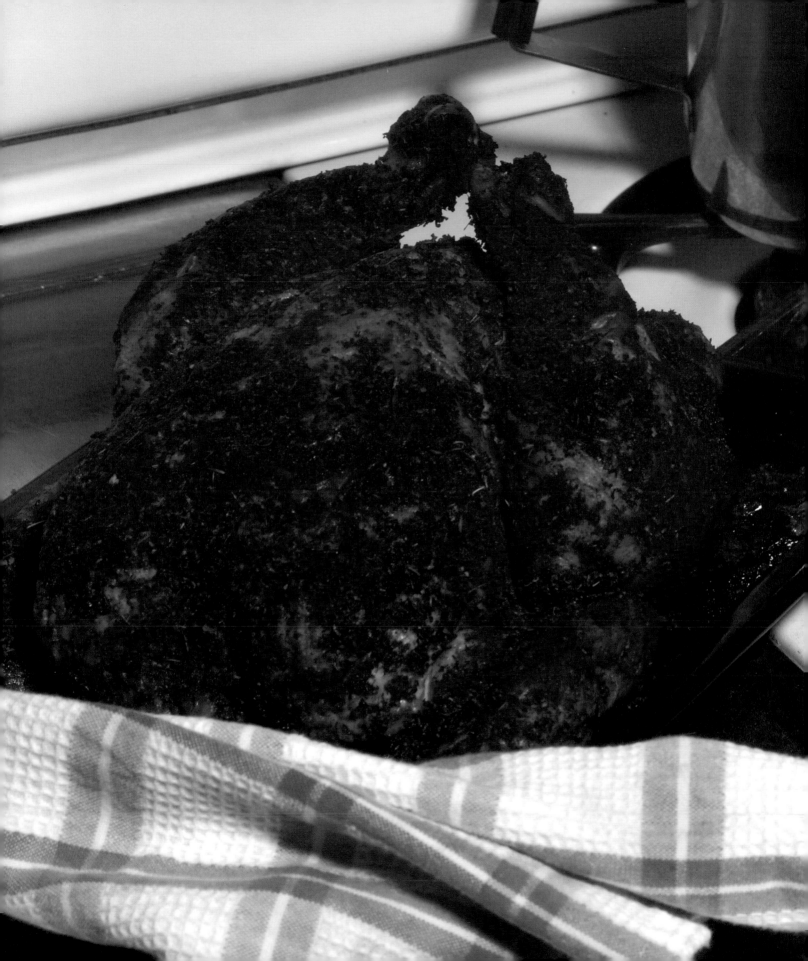

# DUCK MEATBALLS MARINARA

For those who think they don't like duck, or might have had a bad experience in the past with duck, this is the recipe that can bring them back. The rich deep flavor of the duck meat perfectly pairs with the silky, decadent texture and essence of foie gras. This is an easy recipe to use for wild ducks as well, just be sure to clean the breast meat well and remove the skin. **Serves 8 to 10**

Sauce
1 onion, chopped
3 cloves garlic, minced
2 ribs celery
3 tablespoons olive oil
1/2 cup dry red wine
4 cups peeled, seeded, and diced
   tomatoes (canned works well)
2 teaspoons freshly chopped
   oregano
1 teaspoon freshly chopped basil
1/2 teaspoon freshly chopped thyme
1 teaspoon kosher salt
1 pinch freshly ground black pepper

Meatballs
1 pound duck breast, skin on
1 pound pork shoulder
6 ounces foie gras, frozen in chunks
3 tablespoons breadcrumbs
2 tablespoons fresh chopped
   oregano
2 tablespoons fresh chopped thyme
4 cloves garlic, minced
2 eggs
2 tablespoons Dijon mustard
1/2 teaspoon kosher salt
1/4 teaspoon freshly ground black
   pepper
3 quarts canola oil
Freshly grated Parmesan cheese, for
   garnish
Fresh basil, for garnish

### Marinara Sauce
In a large saucepot, sauté the onion, garlic, and celery in olive oil until soft. Deglaze with red wine and reduce until the pan is almost dry. Add tomatoes, bring to a simmer, and purée with a stick blender until smooth. Add the fresh herbs and season with salt and pepper.

### Duck Meatballs
Grind the duck meat, pork shoulder, and frozen foie gras using a grinder plate with the smallest holes. Combine with breadcrumbs, herbs, garlic, eggs, mustard, salt, and pepper in a large mixing bowl and knead together by hand. Cook a small amount in a skillet to check for seasoning level and then roll in 1- to 2-ounce balls. Deep-fry the meatballs in 375-degree F canola oil for 1 minute, or until lightly golden brown on all sides, then place in a large pot and fill with marinara sauce until the meatballs are three-fourths of the way submerged. Simmer covered on low for 12 to 15 minutes, then serve. Garnish with a little grated Parmesan cheese and fresh herbs.

# GRILLED TEXAS QUAIL
# WITH JALAPEÑO CREAM SAUCE

Most commercially raised quail has dark meat, which can be off-putting to any sportsman who's been accustomed to the clean white meat of wild bobwhites. Diamond H birds are light in color, rich in flavor, and always juicy. They elevate raising quail to an art form, keeping the entire operation in house, from egg laying to hatching and incubating. The secret to this recipe is to start with the best quail you can find, then treat them simply and enjoy their naturally good qualities. **Serves 1 to 2**

### Quail
4 fresh thyme sprigs
2 fresh rosemary sprigs
2 fresh cloves garlic, chopped
1/2 teaspoon Bonnell's Creole
   Seasoning Blend (page 182)
2 tablespoons olive oil
2 semiboneless large quail

### Cream Sauce
1 chopped jalapeño, seeded
1 clove garlic, chopped
1/2 teaspoon butter
2 tablespoons dry white wine
1/4 cup heavy cream
Pinch of kosher salt and freshly
   ground black pepper

### Grilled Texas Quail
Remove and discard the stems from all herbs and then chop herbs. Mix the herbs, garlic, seasoning, and oil together and coat the quail both inside and out. Allow to marinate overnight in the refrigerator. Grill over medium heat with a light sprinkle of the seasoning blend until cooked through. Serve hot with Jalapeño Cream Sauce.

### Jalapeño Cream Sauce
Sauté the jalapeños and garlic in butter in a small sauté pan just until the garlic bubbles, but do not brown. Deglaze the pan with wine and reduce until the pan is almost dry. Add the cream and season with salt and pepper. Reduce the sauce until it thickens to a nice rich coating sauce consistency and pour over the quail or serve in a bowl on the side as shown in photo.

# ROASTED STUFFED QUAIL WITH CORNBREAD AND ANDOUILLE SAUSAGE

The sweet nature of the cornbread in this recipe is a natural match for the savory quail and the spicy, smoky sausage. The cornbread stuffing soaks up all of the natural juices of the cooked birds and becomes a complex, flavorful accompaniment to the rich nature of the quail. **Serves 3**

---

1 poblano pepper

1 red bell pepper

1 small onion, finely diced

2 cloves garlic, minced

8 ounces smoked Andouille
    sausage, diced

2 tablespoons butter

2 teaspoons Bonnell's Creole
    Seasoning Blend (page 182)

10–12 ounces cornbread, cut into
    large cubes

1 cup chicken stock

6 semiboneless Texas Quail

Pinch of salt and pepper

1 teaspoon canola oil

Roast the peppers over an open fire until completely black on all sides. Place in a ziplock bag and allow to cool for 10 to 15 minutes. Scrape off the black skins with the back side of a knife blade, then remove the seeds and chop. In a large pan, sauté the onion, garlic, peppers, and sausage in butter until the onions become soft. Add seasoning blend and then the cornbread and stock. Remove from the pan, place in a mixing bowl, and allow the stock to soak into the cornbread. Mix well and then stuff as much mixture as you can into the quail. Season the birds with salt and pepper on the outside and brush well with canola oil; roast in a 425-degree F oven until cooked through. This should take 6 to 8 minutes, but different ovens will vary. To check for doneness, pull one quail leg back to see if the thigh is cooked.

---

# MUSHROOM-STUFFED CHUKAR PARTRIDGE WITH SAGE GRAVY

Chukar partridges are beautiful game birds that can be almost as large as Cornish hens. Their meat is very light and lean. Be careful not to overcook these prized partridges as their rich meat can dry out quickly. **Serves 2**

---

2 shiitake mushrooms
1 oyster mushroom
1 crimini mushroom
1 small shallot, minced
1 clove garlic, minced
1 teaspoon butter
4 tablespoons dry white wine
2 fresh thyme sprigs, chopped
Pinch of kosher salt and freshly
    ground black pepper
1 whole chukar partridge
1 teaspoon canola oil
3 fresh sage leaves
6 tablespoons heavy cream

Clean the mushrooms, remove the stems, and then slice. In a large sauté pan, sweat half of the shallot, the mushrooms, and the garlic in butter until the mushrooms begin to soften. Add in the wine and thyme, then reduce until the pan is almost completely dry. Add salt and pepper, remove from the pan, and cool. Remove the breast meat from each side of the chukar, leaving the skin on, and then cut a small pocket inside each breast portion with a small paring knife. Insert the paring knife lengthwise straight into the breast at the thickest part, but only penetrate just over halfway. Move the knife back and forth to form a little pocket. Stuff the pocket with as much of the mushroom mixture as you can. Season the breast lightly on the outside with salt and pepper then heat a cast-iron pan and sear the outside of the chukar to a golden brown in canola oil. Place the entire pan into a 400-degree F convection oven until a 150-degree F internal temperature is reached and the meat is cooked through. Remove the breasts and set aside to rest. In the same pan, sauté the remaining shallot on high; tear the sage leaves roughly and add to the pan. Add the heavy cream and reduce until a thick gravy has formed. Season with salt and pepper. Just before serving, cut the stuffed breasts in half, plate, and then pour the creamy sage gravy over the top.

---

# QUAIL RAVIOLIS

Raviolis are a labor of love that can add elegance to any dinner party. Bursting with flavor, these delicate raviolis can make even those unaccustomed to wild game at ease. **Yields 16 to 20 large raviolis**

---

### Filling

8 ounces clean boneless quail meat
1 teaspoon olive oil
1 shallot, chopped
2 poblano peppers, roasted, peeled, and seeded
1 red bell pepper, roasted, peeled, and seeded
2 cloves garlic
1/2 teaspoon Bonnell's Southwestern Seasoning Blend (page 181)
3 tablespoons whole pine nuts, lightly toasted
2 teaspoons chopped fresh thyme
2 teaspoons chopped fresh basil
2 eggs

### Cream Sauce

2 tablespoons pine nuts
1 bunch fresh basil, leaves only
2 tablespoons grated Parmesan cheese
1 anchovy fillet
1 small clove garlic
Juice of 2 lemons
1/4 teaspoon salt
2 1/2 tablespoons extra virgin olive oil
2/3 cup heavy cream
Pinch of salt and pepper
Fresh sage leaves (2–3 per serving), for garnish
1 cup canola oil

### Ravioli

4–5 large sheets fresh pasta

### Quail Filling

In a hot sauté pan, brown the quail meat in olive oil. Add the shallot, peppers, and garlic, and cook until the meat is done. Season with seasoning. Add pine nuts and herbs and cool the mixture slightly. Place the mixture in a food processor and pulse a few short times, then add the eggs. Pulse just enough to incorporate the eggs into the mixture; remove and cool the mixture completely. It should still have a somewhat chunky, rough texture. Refrigerate until ready to stuff the ravioli.

### Pesto Cream Sauce

Lightly toast the pine nuts in a small nonstick pan over medium heat until they become very lightly browned on all sides. Remove from the pan. Place the basil, cheese, anchovy, garlic, lemon juice, and salt into a blender. While blending, slowly drizzle in the olive oil until a thick sauce consistency is achieved. Add the pesto and cream to a medium-size saucepan and stir together. Reduce until the mixture reaches a slightly thick sauce consistency. Season with salt and pepper.

Drop the fresh sage leaves into 1 cup of hot canola oil (365 degrees F) and cook until they stop bubbling. Remove and drain on paper towels. Use as garnish on top of Pesto Cream Sauce.

### Ravioli

Cut the pasta sheets into 3- to 4-inch squares and stuff approximately 1 tablespoon of the mixture between 2 squares. Use the tines of a fork to gently press the pasta edges together or crimp together the edges using a pasta wheel. If the pasta has trouble sticking, brush on a little beaten egg to help act as a binder. Refrigerate the ravioli for at least 1 hour to allow them to dry before cooking. Simmer in lightly salted water for 2 to 3 minutes and then serve over Pesto Cream Sauce.

---

# SEARED DUCK BREAST WITH WILD MUSHROOM AND CABERNET DEMIGLACE

Duck is a unique bird with dark red meat, rich intense flavor, and a fatty skin that can make or break the dish. Be sure to render down the skin to get it crispy for that succulent flavor that adds to the meat without being too fatty. Any extra duck fat that renders out in the pan can be saved for cooking other items later. I like to sauté vegetables in duck fat or brown potatoes for hash in it. It also makes the finest roux you've ever tasted. **Serves 2**

---

**Duck Breast**
2 boneless duck breasts, skin on
1/4 teaspoon kosher salt
Pinch of ground black pepper

**Demiglace**
1 small shallot, diced
1/3 cup roughly chopped assorted
   wild mushrooms (I recommend
   chanterelles, shiitakes, oyster, hen
   of the woods, and white trumpets,
   but any mix will work)
1 clove garlic, minced
1/4 cup Cabernet (red wine)
1/4 cup veal demiglace
2 fresh thyme sprigs, stemmed and
   chopped
Pinch of salt and pepper
1 teaspoon butter

**Seared Duck Breast**
Lightly score the skin of each duck breast in a crisscross pattern, then season well with salt and pepper on both sides. Place in a dry medium-hot skillet, skin side down, without using any oil. As the skin begins to render off the fat, the meat will slowly start to cook on that side. Cook with the skin side down until the meat is almost cooked to your desired temperature (I recommend medium-rare or 130 degrees F). Turn over and brown the meat side in the duck fat, and then remove the breast from the pan and allow to rest while making the sauce. Pour off most of the fat from the pan.

**Wild Mushroom and Cabernet Demiglace**
Saute the shallot, mushrooms, and garlic in remaining duck fat until the mushrooms begin to give off some of their liquid. Add the wine and reduce until the pan is almost dry. Add the demiglace and thyme and season with salt and pepper. Slice the duck breasts into long thin strips (cutting directly across the grain of the meat) and arrange on a dinner plate. Add the butter to the sauce and swirl the pan just until the butter melts, then serve over the duck immediately.

---

# SMOKED WILD TURKEY

The legs of a wild bird will not be tender enough to eat when using this recipe, so I usually reserve them for later. I like to make a soup by simmering the legs gently for an additional 2 to 3 hours in chicken stock with aromatic vegetables until the meat is tender enough to be pulled easily from the bones, then chopped and returned to the soup. **Serves 8 to 10**

1 (10- to 12-pound) whole wild turkey
2 gallons water
1½ pints honey
1½ pints kosher salt
5 pounds ice
4 oranges
20 bay leaves
1 bottle dry white wine
¼ cup black peppercorns
10–12 strips of bacon
4 tablespoons salt
1 tablespoon pepper

Clean the bird of any excess feathers and thoroughly rinse the inside of the body cavity. Bring the water to a light simmer and add the honey and salt to make a basic brine. As soon as the salt and honey have dissolved, pour the brine over ice to cool before soaking the bird. Cut the oranges in half, squeeze them, and drop in the brine. Add all remaining ingredients (except the bacon, and remaining salt and pepper) and then submerge the turkey in the brine and allow to soak overnight in the refrigerator. Remove the bird from the brine the next day and sprinkle the inside of the cavity with salt and pepper. Place strips of bacon over the breast and smoke over pecan wood chips at 250 degrees F for approximately 3 hours. When the turkey is done, pull back the skin from the breast meat and slice the meat very thinly across the grain to serve.

# SOUTHWESTERN CHICKEN STACK

This is what happens when chicken enchiladas grow up and get an education. I love the complexity of this dish and diversity of textures, temperatures, and spices. It takes a little labor to create, but the final product takes comfort food Tex-Mex to an entirely new level. **Serves 1**

4 ounces pulled smoked free-range
   chicken (page 92)
1/2 teaspoon butter
1/4 cup Pico de Gallo (page 16)
3 corn tortillas
1 cup canola oil
2 tablespoons Salsa Verde
3 tablespoons Guajillo Chile Sauce
   (page 84)
2 tablespoons grated queso fresco
1 grilled free-range chicken breast
1 tablespoon sour cream
1/4 cup Guacamole (see page 34)

Salsa Verde
5 pounds tomatillos
1 large onion
2 jalapeños
3 cloves garlic
1 quart chicken stock
2 limes
1 bunch cilantro
Salt and pepper

In a hot sauté pan, quickly heat the pulled smoked chicken in butter with half of the Pico de Gallo just until warm. The chicken has already been cooked, so this step should be done quickly so as not to overcook and dry out the chicken. Dip the corn tortillas in hot oil (375 degrees F) for a few seconds just until soft; drain on paper towels and place in a bowl. Cover the tortillas in salsa verde to coat both sides thoroughly. Begin the presentation by pouring a layer of hot guajillo sauce on the bottom of the plate. Place a warm salsa-coated tortilla in the center; put half of the smoked chicken mix on top. Sprinkle with half of the queso fresco and place another tortilla on top. Add another layer of smoked chicken, the rest of the queso fresco, and top with the third tortilla. Slice the grilled chicken breast into thirds and arrange on top. Garnish the stack with the remaining pico, sour cream, and guacamole and serve.

**Salsa Verde**
Roast the tomatillos over an open flame until brown on all sides. Saute onion, jalapeños, and garlic, and then add tomatillos and chicken stock; simmer for 30 minutes. Puree in a food processor or blender and then add lime juice, cilantro, and salt and pepper to taste.

# PHEASANT STUFFED WITH GOAT CHEESE AND HERBS IN PHYLLO

This is an easy dish to make a day ahead, and it will keep very well in the refrigerator. Bake at the last minute and be sure to get the outer phyllo pastry golden brown and flaky. The cooking time may vary quite a bit, depending on the size of the pheasant, but it's easy to check the internal temperature with a thermometer without having to cut in to see if it's done. When the middle reaches 140 to 145 degrees F, it's ready. **Serves 1 to 2**

1/3 cup fresh goat cheese
2 tablespoons chopped shallot
2 thyme sprigs
2 sage leaves
1/4 teaspoon chopped rosemary
Pinch of kosher salt and freshly
    ground black pepper
2 (4-ounce) pheasant breasts
2–3 strips roasted red pepper
6 tablespoons butter
8 sheets phyllo dough

Combine the goat cheese, shallot, and herbs in a mixing bowl and season with salt and pepper. Remove the skin from the pheasant breasts and pound breasts down to a thin, uniform thickness. Smother the entire surface with the goat cheese mixture. Place one or two strips of red pepper in the middle, then roll the pheasant breasts up into a roulade (like a jellyroll). Melt the butter. Lay one sheet of phyllo dough on a smooth counter surface; brush well with melted butter. Lay down a second sheet on top and brush again. Repeat until four layers of the phyllo have been buttered. Place one pheasant roulade on the dough and roll from one end to the other, folding in the ends to create a somewhat sealed package. Be sure there is enough butter to help keep the dough together and refrigerate. Repeat for the second pheasant breast as well. Preheat an oven to 400 degrees F, and cook the stuffed pheasant on parchment paper or a nonstick surface for approximately 15 to 18 minutes. The time may vary, depending on the thickness of the pheasant and the type of oven being used. The outside should become golden brown and the pheasant should be cooked just through. Remove from the oven and allow to cool for 2 to 3 minutes before slicing. Cut on the bias and serve hot.

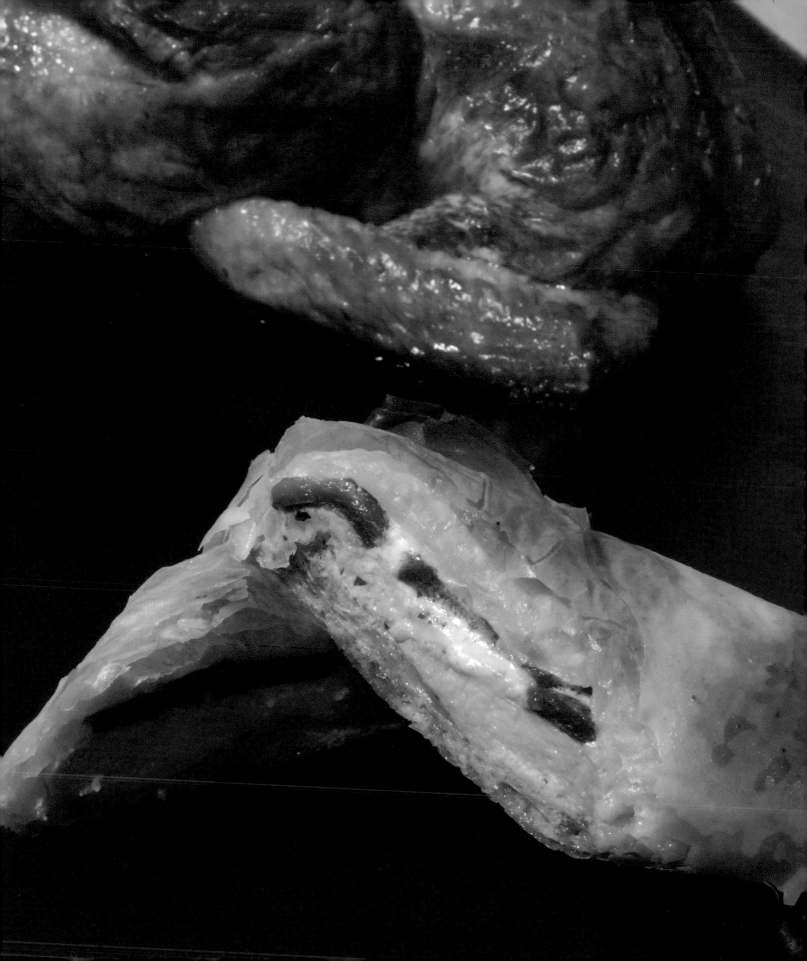

# WILD GAME

★ ★ ★

★ Bone-In Cowboy-Cut Buffalo Rib-Eye with Crispy 1015 Tobacco Onions ★
★ Buffalo Tenderloin Peppersteak with Smoked Whiskey Cream Sauce ★
★ Buffalo Rib-Eye in Puff Pastry with Cognac Sauce ★
★ Elk Tenderloin with Yellow Tomato Sauce ★
★ Seared Lamb with Mac 'n' Goat Cheese and Lemon-Dressed Watercress ★
★ Rack of Blackbuck Antelope with Wild Mushroom and Dijon Mustard Sauce ★
★ Rack of Wild Boar with Pomegranate Rum Sauce ★
★ Rocky Mountain Elk Chop with Sherry Demiglaze ★
★ Seared Axis Venison Loin with Shiitake Jalapeño Cream Sauce ★
★ Smoked Chili-Crusted Buffalo Sandwich with Horseradish Cream ★
★ Texas Ostrich Fan Fillet with Sherry-Laced Mushrooms ★ Venison Cheese Steak ★

---

Wild game will always bring back great memories of growing up in the outdoors with my brother and my dad. Since we always managed to have something wild in the freezer, it was only natural that my brother and I constantly pestered and pleaded with my dad to cook something that we had harvested for the next family dinner. Probably the most experimental we ever got in the kitchen while growing up stemmed from looking at a sink filled with three ducks, six quail, and one venison backstrap. That's when we were forced into creative thought and explored every preparation method possible to try and convince the rest of the family or invited guests to taste the bounty from our latest conquest. It's quite a proud moment for a young teenager to harvest game and then see the truly surprised faces of dinner guests muttering something like, "You know I usually don't like venison, but this is really good. What's your recipe?" as they clean their plates and ask for seconds. Some dishes were quite successful, while others failed to pass even our own taste and smell test; but, nonetheless, I learned a tremendous amount about cooking wild game and about the challenges and rewards of such endeavors from a young age.

As a culinary student, eager to reach the status of "classically trained chef," I again kept pestering the chef instructors of the New England Culinary Institute to teach us something about wild game cooking. Any time it was my turn to create a nightly special in one of the school's restaurants, I was always seeking out some buffalo, venison, or other type of "oddity" to most New Englanders. Every dish received great reviews from the few rare customers who dared to step out of their comfort zone and try something so obscure for this neck of the woods. As soon as I moved back to Texas, I found a much more adventurous and trusting crowd of diners. Here in Fort Worth, venison, antelope, elk, and buffalo now literally fly out of my kitchen. I certainly love beef, and would never dream of having a steak-free restaurant; but with wild game, there is simply so much more to try. Cooking game (and, more importantly, cleaning game) can be a tricky challenge to take on. The temperature range for cooking game requires pinpoint accuracy with a very narrow window of cooking time separating completely raw from bone-dry, but the rewards of perfectly cooked medium-rare elk tenderloin are tremendous. Each game meat has a flavor and texture all its own, and those unique and bold flavors can be coaxed into something almost magical if skillfully prepared. ★

*Buffalo Tenderloin Peppersteak with Smoked Whiskey Cream Sauce, recipe on page 115.*

# BONE-IN COWBOY-CUT BUFFALO RIB-EYE WITH CRISPY 1015 TOBACCO ONIONS

This tends to be one of those "everything's bigger in Texas" kind of dishes. This particular cut of buffalo usually ranges from 35 to 48 ounces per steak! It's a real crowd-pleaser for its visual appeal, but the meat is also exceptional and usually well-marbled. The side dish is called tobacco onions because they look liked shredded tobacco after they are prepared. **Serves 2 to 4**

4 tablespoons Bonnell's
    Southwestern Seasoning Blend
    (page 181)
1¹/₂ tablespoons kosher salt
2 large bone-in buffalo rib-eye
    steaks
Texas 1015 Tobacco Onions (page
    172)

Combine the seasonings and pour them onto the rib-eyes, rubbing thoroughly into the meat. Allow the seasonings to penetrate for 1 hour before cooking. Cook the steaks over a hardwood fire on the hottest part of the grill to get good dark grill marks on the outside of the meat. After that, move the steaks to the coolest part of the grill and either pull the lid down or cover with an upside-down pan to create an oven around the meat. The steaks should be cooked to medium-rare, about 18 to 20 minutes (130 degrees F internal), depending on the grill temperature. They can also be finished in an oven, but the flavor of the wood grill won't be quite as prominent. Allow to rest for at least 5 minutes before cutting into the meat to prevent all of the juices from running out. Pile each steak high with Crispy 1015 Tobacco Onions and serve.

# BUFFALO TENDERLOIN PEPPERSTEAK WITH SMOKED WHISKEY CREAM SAUCE

This is one of the most popular dishes I've ever served. Though technically not true buffalo, American bison meat is similar in anatomy to beef but is much richer. It really takes well to generous amounts of black pepper, and I love to pair it with the sweet nature of this unique mesquite-aged whiskey in a luxurious cream sauce. **Serves 1** *(photo on page 113)*

---

¼ teaspoon kosher salt
1 teaspoon cracked black pepper
1 (8–9-ounce) buffalo fillet
1 teaspoon canola oil
1 tablespoon butter
1 small shallot, finely chopped
1 clove garlic, chopped
2 tablespoons plus 1½ teaspoons McKendrick's Mesquite-Aged Whiskey (Jack Daniel's plus 1 drop liquid smoke may be substituted)
¼ cup heavy cream

Mix the salt and pepper together, and spread out on a large plate. Press the fillet down in the seasonings to coat on both flat sides thoroughly. In a medium-size hot skillet, brown the steak on all sides in canola oil. Place the pan and steak in a 350-degree F oven and finish cooking until desired temperature is reached (130 degrees F, medium-rare recommended, about 6 to 10 minutes). Remove steak from pan and allow to rest while finishing the sauce. In the same pan, add the butter, shallot, and garlic. Sauté until lightly brown and then add the whiskey. Be careful to do this away from the flame, because the whiskey will flame. If using an electric range, light with a match and stand back. After whiskey has burned out, add the cream and reduce to a slightly thick consistency that will coat the steak. Pour the sauce directly over the cooked fillet, allowing the sauce to run down all sides and serve.

---

# BUFFALO RIB-EYE IN PUFF PASTRY WITH COGNAC SAUCE

Puff pastry is a great multitasking ingredient in this dish. Not only does it provide a fancy presentation bowl, but it also acts as a delicious accompaniment that helps soak up all the sweet, savory sauce. **Serves 2**

---

**Bowls**
2 sheets puff pastry
1 egg yolk, beaten

**Sauce**
12 ounces buffalo rib-eye, cubed
1 teaspoon canola oil
1 teaspoon butter
2 pinches of kosher salt
Pinch of freshly ground black pepper
2 tablespoons chopped shallot
1/2 cup sliced shiitake mushrooms
   (no stems)
1/4 cup quartered button mushrooms
1 clove garlic, minced
1/4 cup cognac
3 sprigs fresh thyme, stemmed
1/4 cup heavy cream

**Puff Pastry Bowls**
Cut one large circle out of the puff pastry and place on a baking sheet lined with parchment paper. Cut another circle of the same diameter; in that circle, cut out another circle that is one inch smaller to form a ring of pastry. Using a little egg yolk as a binder, place the ring of puff pastry directly on top of the first circle of puff pastry, then brush the entire thing with a light coating of egg yolk. Repeat this process to form another puff pastry bowl just like the first one. Place in a 400-degree F oven and cook until the pastries have risen completely and are browned on top, about 10 minutes (but times will vary with different pastries and different ovens). Remove the pastry bowls. The bottom layer will have puffed up into the center. To deepen the bowl, cut out the center with a sharp knife and reserve for later.

**Buffalo Rib-Eye in Cognac Sauce**
In a large skillet, brown the buffalo cubes in a mixture of canola oil and butter, and season with a pinch of salt and pepper. Once the meat has browned, add shallot, mushrooms, and garlic, and cook until the mushrooms begin to soften. Deglaze the pan with cognac and allow to flame off. When the cognac has reduced to almost a dry pan, add the thyme and cream, and reduce until the cream begins to thicken. Season once again with another pinch of salt and then pour the mixture into the puff pastry bowls. Top each one with the circle of puff pastry cut from the middles and serve.

---

★ **WARNING!** Do not pour any liquor directly from a bottle into a hot pan. It is possible for the bottle to ignite and explode. Any time you cook with liquor, pour the desired amount into a glass and pour from the glass into a pan.

# ELK TENDERLOIN
# WITH YELLOW TOMATO SAUCE

Elk is one of the sweetest flavored of all the game meats. It's very easy to like, and the wild meat tastes very similar to the commercially available meat, unless the elk comes from an area with an abundance of sagebrush, which can impart a strong sage flavor throughout the meat. Just like all other game meats, do not overcook. Anything past medium will dry it out in a hurry. **Serves 3**

---

**Sauce**
2 shallots, minced
2 cloves garlic, minced
2 teaspoons extra virgin olive oil
2 large yellow beefsteak tomatoes,
　roughly chopped
1 cup chicken stock
Pinch of dried chipotle powder
¼ teaspoon kosher salt
½ lemon, to finish

**Tenderloin**
3 (6-ounce) fresh elk tenderloin
　portions
½ teaspoon kosher salt
Pinch of freshly ground black pepper
1 teaspoon canola oil

**Yellow Tomato Sauce**
In a medium-size saucepan, sauté the shallots and garlic in olive oil briefly, then add all remaining ingredients and simmer for 18 to 20 minutes. Purée with a stick blender and strain. If the sauce appears too thin, reduce until slightly thick. If the sauce is too thick, add a touch more chicken stock. The idea is to achieve a sauce with just enough thickness to coat the back of a spoon. Finish with a squeeze of fresh lemon juice.

**Elk Tenderloin**
Cut each elk tenderloin into 3 medallions and season on all sides with salt and pepper. Brush lightly with canola oil to prevent the meat from sticking to the grill. Over very high heat, grill the elk quickly on each side until the meat just reaches medium rare. Depending on the thickness of the elk, this can usually be done in about 1 to 1½ minutes per side. To serve, spoon a couple of tablespoons sauce onto each dinner plate, and arrange 3 medallions on top of the sauce.

---

# SEARED LAMB WITH MAC 'N' GOAT CHEESE AND LEMON-DRESSED WATERCRESS

Lamb and goat cheese are naturally great flavors together. I love putting comfort foods like mac 'n' cheese in a fine presentation. It's a way of dressing it up, or making fancy fare more approachable, depending on how you look at it.
Serves 1

---

**Mac 'n' Goat Cheese**
1 tablespoon butter
1 tablespoon flour
1½ cups goat's milk
Pinch of kosher salt and white
    pepper
1 small jalapeño pepper, seeded and
    finely diced
½ Roma tomato, seeded and finely
    diced
2 tablespoons crumbled fresh goat
    cheese
1 cup cooked small pasta shells

**Lamb**
6–7 ounces boneless lamb loin
2 pinches of kosher salt
1 teaspoon canola oil
½ cup red wine
1 tablespoon veal demiglace
    (available in gourmet stores)
¼ teaspoon butter
Pinch of pepper

**Garnish**
1 small bunch fresh watercress
½ tablespoon fresh lemon juice
1 tablespoon extra virgin olive oil
1 tablespoon crumbled goat cheese
Salt and pepper, to taste

**Mac 'n' Goat Cheese**
Add the butter and flour together in a medium saucepan and whisk together over low to medium heat until a roux has formed. Do not cook until brown, just to the stage where the butter begins to cook the flour and it starts to smell like sourdough toast. Remove from pan and set aside. Add the goat's milk to the pan and season with salt and pepper. Reduce by one-third and then add the cooled roux. Whisk together and bring to a simmer. The sauce will thicken when it starts to simmer. If the sauce is too thick, add a little more milk. If it's too thin, reduce more. Add the jalapeño, tomato, cheese, and pasta, and stir together. Check for seasonings and use a ring mold to plate.

**Seared Lamb**
Season the lamb loin with salt on all sides, then sear in a medium-size hot sauté pan in just a touch of canola oil. Brown on all sides and cook until desired temperature is reached (130 degrees F for medium-rare, about 4 to 6 minutes). Allow the meat to rest for 2 to 3 minutes before slicing into medallions. Plate with Mac 'n' Goat Cheese, and then top with lemony watercress greens. In the same pan, deglaze with red wine and reduce until the pan is almost dry. Add the demiglace, mount with a dab of butter, and swirl just until the butter is completely melted. Season with a pinch of salt and pepper. Pour the sauce over the lamb medallions just before serving.

**Garnish**
At the last possible moment, dress the watercress greens with lemon juice and olive oil in a mixing bowl. Add a few pieces of goat cheese and then place on top of or next to the Mac 'n' Goat Cheese. If this step is done too far ahead, the watercress will wilt.

---

# RACK OF BLACKBUCK ANTELOPE WITH WILD MUSHROOM AND DIJON MUSTARD SAUCE

Blackbuck antelope are very common in the Hill Country of Texas, and their meat is one of the most highly prized varieties of venison anywhere. Although not native to Texas, there are more blackbucks in Texas now that anywhere else in the world. **Serves 4**

---

### Sauce
1 small shallot, minced

1 clove garlic, minced

3 ounces assorted wild mushrooms (I like morels, chanterelles, and black trumpet mushrooms, but they can be quite seasonal; shiitakes, criminis, and oysters will also work and are more easily available)

1 tablespoon butter

$\frac{1}{2}$ teaspoon kosher salt

Pinch of freshly ground black pepper

$1\frac{1}{2}$ tablespoons heavy cream

2 teaspoons demiglace

$\frac{1}{2}$ teaspoon chopped fresh marjoram

1 tablespoon Dijon mustard

### Antelope
2 whole blackbuck antelope racks (usually 7–8 bones)

2–3 teaspoons kosher salt

$1\frac{1}{2}$ tablespoons canola oil

1 tablespoon Dijon mustard

### Wild Mushroom and Dijon Mustard Sauce
In a medium nonstick pan, sweat the shallot, garlic, and mushrooms in butter for 1 to 2 minutes. Do not overcook the wild mushrooms or they will lose much of their unique flavors. Season the mix with salt and pepper, and then add heavy cream and demiglace. Swirl the pan until the sauce takes on a uniform color. Right before serving, add the marjoram and mustard, and swirl together.

### Blackbuck Antelope
Season the racks of blackbuck on all sides with salt. Rub it thoroughly into all parts of the meat and between the bones. Heat a medium cast-iron skillet until it begins to smoke. Drizzle in canola oil and brown the racks on all sides. Once the outsides are browned, remove and drain on paper towels. They should be well browned on the outside but still raw in the middle. Rub the racks while still slightly warm with Dijon mustard and allow to marinate in the fridge for at least 2 hours. Once the racks have finished marinating, roast in a 425-degree F oven until medium-rare. Time will vary depending on the size of the racks and your particular oven, but be careful not to overcook. Use an instant-read thermometer and pull out the meat when the internal temperature reaches 125 degrees F. Allow the meat to rest for 3 to 4 minutes before cutting the chops apart. This will help keep the juices from flowing all over the cutting board. Slice the blackbuck into individual chops, arrange on a plate, and then top with the sauce just before serving.

---

# RACK OF WILD BOAR WITH POMEGRANATE RUM SAUCE

Wild boar in Texas is more plentiful than we would like it to be. The meat is similar to pork, but leaner and much richer.
**Serves 2**

---

**Sauce**
1 tablespoon chopped shallot
1 clove garlic, chopped
1 teaspoon canola oil
4 tablespoons rum
8–10 pomegranate seeds
1/2 teaspoon pomegranate molasses
1 1/2 tablespoons veal demiglace
Pinch of kosher salt
1 tablespoon butter

**Wild Boar**
1 frenched wild boar rack
1 tablespoon Bonnell's Southwestern
    Seasoning Blend (page 181)

**Pomegranate Rum Sauce**
In a medium saucepan, sauté the shallot and garlic in canola oil for 1 minute. Add the rum and allow to flame off; then add all remaining ingredients, except the butter, and simmer together until the sauce thickens slightly. Add the butter and swirl until the butter is melted and incorporated into the velvety rich sauce.

For an added degree of flare, add 1 tablespoon 151-proof rum at the last second to the pomegranate sauce while in the pan. Flame and pour over the chops. Be careful doing this step, as serving flaming dishes can be quite dangerous. Never pour alcohol directly from a bottle into a hot pan. Pour from a glass instead.

**Rack of Wild Boar**
Rub the rack of wild boar thoroughly on all sides with the seasoning and allow to marinate for 1 hour. Roast the boar in a 375-degree F convection oven until the internal temperature reaches 130 degrees F. Remove from the oven and allow to rest 4 to 5 minutes before cutting. Slice the boar rack into individual chops and pour over the sauce over the boar just before serving.

---

# ROCKY MOUNTAIN ELK CHOP WITH SHERRY DEMIGLAZE

If you're lucky enough to find it, fresh elk is a real treat. This dish pairs extremely well with Cabernet Sauvignon or Syrah. **Serves 2**

½ teaspoon kosher salt, plus a pinch
   for the sauce
¼ teaspoon freshly ground black
   pepper, plus a pinch for the sauce
2 cleaned elk rib chops
1 teaspoon canola oil
1 small shallot, minced
1 clove garlic
6 tablespoons dry cream sherry
2 tablespoons demiglace
2 tablespoons butter

Combine the salt and pepper together and season the elk chops thoroughly on all sides. In a large hot cast-iron pan, brown the chops well on all sides in canola oil, then place the entire pan into a 400-degree F oven to finish cooking. Cook to an internal temperature of 130 degrees F, then remove the pan from the oven and set the chops on a warm plate to rest while making the sauce. In the same pan, sweat the shallot and garlic, add the sherry, and allow to flame off. Let the sherry reduce until the pan is almost dry and then add the demiglace. Once the demiglace is fully incorporated, add the butter and swirl until it has melted into the sauce. Season with a pinch of salt and pepper, pour over the chops, and serve.

# SEARED AXIS VENISON LOIN WITH SHIITAKE JALAPEÑO CREAM SAUCE

This is a simple dish that can be made start to finish in under 10 minutes. The quality of this dish will be completely determined by the quality and freshness of the venison and the cooking temperature. I like to cook these medallions for just under one minute per side in a very hot pan, just enough to brown each side and leave the middle medium-rare. **Serves 1**

---

3 (1-inch-thick) axis venison backstrap medallions

Pinch of kosher salt, for meat and sauce

Pinch of ground black pepper, for meat and sauce

1 teaspoon canola oil

1 cup thinly sliced shiitake mushrooms

1 fresh jalapeño, seeded and chopped

1 clove garlic, minced

1 splash dry white wine

½ cup heavy cream

Clean the venison well of all sinew, fat, or silverskin. Pound each medallion to ½ inch thick with your hand. Season both sides with a pinch of salt and pepper and brown both sides in a medium-size very hot skillet in canola oil. Remove from pan and set aside. The meat should be a perfect medium-rare at this point. Using the same pan, add the mushrooms and jalapeño, and sauté until they become soft. Add the garlic for the last minute, but do not brown or it will become bitter. Add wine and then reduce until the pan is almost dry. Add the cream, season with a pinch of salt and pepper, and then reduce until the sauce becomes slightly thick. Pour over the medallions of venison while hot and serve.

---

★ **TIP:** For even richer flavor, add a pinch of fresh thyme to the cream.

# SMOKED CHILI-CRUSTED BUFFALO SANDWICH WITH HORSERADISH CREAM

This is a great dish for helping anyone learn to like game. Buffalo meat is very lean, has a very mild flavor, and really absorbs smoky flavors well. **Serves 8**

---

**Cream**

¼ cup mayonnaise

2 tablespoons sour cream

2½ tablespoons prepared
    horseradish

½ teaspoon lemon juice

Pinch of kosher salt, cayenne pepper,
    and white pepper

**Sandwich**

2 pounds buffalo eye round
    (tenderloin will work, but is much
    more expensive)

2 tablespoons Bonnell's Creole
    Seasoning Blend (page 182)

8 toasted rolls

**Horseradish Cream**

Combine all of the ingredients and chill until ready to use.

**Smoked Chili-Crusted Buffalo Sandwich**

Dry-rub the eye round with seasoning on all sides and allow to marinate for 1 to 2 hours in the refrigerator. Preheat a smoker to 225 degrees F using pecan wood. Set the buffalo in the smoker and cook until the internal temperature reaches 130 degrees F, remove, wrap tightly with plastic wrap, and refrigerate overnight. When ready to serve, shave the thinnest possible slices across the grain of the meat. If thick slices are cut, this meat will definitely be tough, but if shaved thin, it's tender and delicious. The best method is to use a deli slicer. Mound 4 ounces of the shaved buffalo meat onto your favorite toasted roll and spread with horseradish cream.

---

# TEXAS OSTRICH FAN FILLET WITH SHERRY-LACED MUSHROOMS

The fan fillet of ostrich is my favorite cut in the entire bird, including the pricey tenderloins. It's one particular muscle from the leg that is incredibly tender and exceptionally lean. Ostrich is a rich dark-red meat throughout and is closer in taste to venison than any type of bird. **Serves 1**

1 (8-ounce) ostrich fan fillet
Pinch of kosher salt, plus more
  for sauce
Pinch of freshly ground black
  pepper, plus more for sauce
1 teaspoon canola oil
Sherry-Laced Mushrooms (page 180)

Season the ostrich fillet on all sides with salt and pepper, and then brush lightly with canola oil to prevent it from sticking to the grill. Grill over high heat until an internal temperature reaches 130 degrees F, about 6 to 8 minutes. Remove from the grill and place on a warm dinner plate to rest. Spoon Sherry-Laced Mushrooms over the top and serve.

# VENISON CHEESE STEAK

This is a great dish for kids or beginners who might be slightly squeamish about trying venison for the first time.
**Serves 3**

1 pound lean venison

1½ teaspoons Bonnell's Southwestern Seasoning Blend (page 181), plus ⅓ teaspoon for dusting peppers

1 red bell pepper

2 jalapeño peppers

1 large Texas 1015 onion, julienned

2 tablespoons canola oil

3 hoagie rolls

5 slices fontina cheese

Clean any sinew, silverskin, or fat from the venison until only lean meat remains. Slice the venison into extremely thin strips using a sharp knife. Dust liberally with the seasoning and allow the rub to marinate and soak into the meat for at least 5 to 8 minutes before cooking. Roast the bell pepper and jalapeños over an open flame until the skins turn black on all sides. Place in a ziplock bag and allow to sweat for 10 to 15 minutes, or until cool enough to handle. Remove the skins from the peppers using the back side of a knife blade to scrape off the black charred outer layer. Remove the stems and seeds, then slice into long thin strips. Dust the onion with ⅓ teaspoon seasoning blend and sauté in oil until the strips are well caramelized and browned. Remove and combine the onion and peppers together. Heat a medium cast-iron skillet until it begins to smoke and then drizzle in canola oil and sear the venison on all sides. The pan should be hot enough that the thin venison strips can brown on both sides in about 1 minute at the most. Each strip of meat should be cooked very quickly, then set aside on a plate and kept warm. Once all of the venison is cooked, toast the hoagie rolls and fill each one with venison and the onion and pepper mixture; top with a fontina cheese slice. The venison and peppers should be just hot enough to melt the cheese.

# BEEF AND PORK

★ Andouille Sausage ★

★ Andouille-Stuffed Pork Tenderloin with Creole Cream Sauce ★

★ Beef Tenderloin with Poblano Tasso Cream Sauce ★

★ Goat Cheese and Pine Nut–Crusted Beef Tenderloin ★

★ Beef Tenderloin Tower with Cilantro Pesto ★

★ Grass-Fed Texas Rib-Eye with Three-Pepper Compound Butter ★

★ Mesquite-Smoked, Chile-Rubbed Rotisserie Prime Rib ★

★ Sirloin Summer Steak Topped with Seared Avocado and Smoky Salsa ★

★ Smoked Pork Chops with Jack Daniel's and Granny Smith Apple Cider Reduction Sauce ★

★ Smoked Pork Loin Sandwich with Sun-Dried Tomato Cream Sauce ★

Make no mistake, even with all of the wild game and abundance of seafood available to our great state, beef still reigns as the undisputed king of Texas cuisine and probably always will. Nobody ever says "let's go celebrate tonight with a big chicken dinner." When it's time to treat ourselves, we Texans love beef. The hard part for a chef, however, is that most Texans can cook a steak at home. The challenge is to make a steak that tastes great, with just enough imagination and creativity to be on a fine dining menu, but not so much that it no longer resembles a steak. As is the case with most foods, a great steak starts with the highest quality ingredients. I've found one particular supplier who creates the richest tasting beef I've ever used by grass-feeding genetically pure cattle on lush pastures, hand-selecting the cattle when they are at their best, and dry aging all of their cuts. Burgundy Pasture Beef in Grandview, Texas, supplies me with the finest all-natural beef rib-eyes in Texas. Their grass-fed dry-aged meat for hamburgers bursts with rich flavor. The quality of the beef you start with will always dictate just how good the final product can be, so choose wisely and apply time-honored cooking techniques to make a truly great steak.

Even though Texas barbecue is primarily based on beef brisket, pork certainly plays a major role in the Texas food scene. I can hardly imagine a world without pork chops, ham, or bacon. Pork products are such staples in the Texas kitchen, they are often overlooked as a category all their own. One of my earliest pork creations is the Andouille sausage–stuffed pork tenderloin, which really transforms a common cut of pork into an impressive formal dish. I remember serving this dish to my family before I opened my restaurant, and they raved so much that I just had to put it on my opening menu. ★

*Beef Tenderloin Tower with Cilantro Pesto, recipe on page 145.*

# ANDOUILLE SAUSAGE

It's a big undertaking to make your own fresh sausage at home, but if you saw how most of it is made commercially, you'd probably do it yourself much more often. This Andouille makes a great breakfast sausage, but it can also be stuffed into casings and served as links. **Serves 10**

2½ pounds pork shoulder (do not trim the fat)

1¼ tablespoons Bonnell's Creole Seasoning Blend (page 182)

½ pound wild game meat trimmings (lean red meats only: venison, buffalo, etc.)

½ pound sweet onions

3 cloves garlic, chopped

¾ teaspoon cayenne pepper

1 tablespoon kosher salt

½ teaspoon ground mace

⅓ teaspoon dried thyme

Pinch of powdered cloves

⅓ teaspoon allspice

½ teaspoon dried marjoram

1 teaspoon sugar

¼ cup powdered milk

2 teaspoons brandy

Cut the pork shoulder into large chunks. Rub the seasoning into the pork and game meat. Smoke the pork and game meat at 225 degrees F in a pecan wood smoker for 20 minutes. Roughly chop the onions and garlic, and then combine with all remaining ingredients in a large mixing bowl. Mix the seasoned meat with the mixture, cover with plastic wrap, and leave in the refrigerator overnight. On the following day, grind all ingredients together using the fine plate on the grinder. Place the meat into a mixer and beat together with the paddle attachment until well combined. Cook one small portion and taste for seasonings. If the seasoning tastes right, form into 2½-ounce patties and cook over a grill or sauté in a nonstick pan. Serve with quail eggs, sunny side up, for a true Texas ranch breakfast.

# ANDOUILLE-STUFFED PORK TENDERLOIN WITH CREOLE CREAM SAUCE

This stuffing technique, although quite simple, will make you look like a culinary genius. It's also a great way to get rich flavor and seasoning throughout the meat. **Serves 8**

---

**Sauce**
**Creole Sauce (page 88)**
**¹/₂ cup heavy cream**

**Tenderloin**
**1 large link smoked Andouille sausage**
**4 whole pork tenderloins**
**2 teaspoons Bonnell's Southwestern Seasoning Blend (page 181)**

**Creole Cream Sauce**
Combine ingredients and bring to a boil. Reduce to simmer, then serve.

**Andouille-Stuffed Pork Tenderloin**
Cut the link of sausage into quarters lengthwise to form 4 long triangle-shaped sausage sticks. Place them on a plate and freeze until solid. Pierce a hole horizontally through the middle of each pork tenderloin with a knife-sharpening steel. Remove the steel and insert one stick of sausage into the hole, pushing through the entire length of the pork. Try to insert the sausage as close to the center of the pork as possible. Allow the sausage to thaw before cooking the pork. It may be easier to cut the pork tenderloins and sausage links in half before inserting; but with a little practice, you will be able to stuff the pork either way. Rub the pork thoroughly on all sides with the seasoning, then grill or roast to desired temperature with the sausage inside. Once cooked, allow the meat to rest for 3 to 4 minutes and then slice into medallions to show off that stuffed sausage center. Serve with the cream sauce.

---

# BEEF TENDERLOIN WITH POBLANO TASSO CREAM SAUCE

Beef tenderloin is the most luxurious cut available. I love to give it a little spice, so I blanket it in a rich, creamy sauce. It's a perfect dish for special occasions when you just need to really treat yourself. **Serves 2**

2 (8-ounce) tenderloin steaks
¼ teaspoon kosher salt
⅛ teaspoon freshly ground
   black pepper
1½ teaspoons canola oil
2 tablespoons diced tasso ham
1 tablespoon chopped shallot
1 poblano pepper, roasted, peeled,
   seeded, and chopped
1 clove garlic, chopped
4 tablespoons dry white wine
8 tablespoons heavy cream
Pinch of Bonnell's Creole Seasoning
   Blend (page 182)

Season the steaks with salt and pepper on all sides. In a very hot medium-size sauté pan, sear steaks in canola oil until well browned on all sides. Place entire pan in 375-degree F convection oven and cook to desired doneness (130 degrees F for medium-rare, about 8 to 10 minutes). Remove the pan from the oven and set the steaks aside to rest. In the same pan (without washing), add the tasso ham, shallot, pepper, and garlic, and cook until the garlic begins to sizzle; do not brown. Deglaze the pan with wine and reduce until the pan is almost dry. Add the cream and dust with seasoning blend to taste. Reduce until the cream thickens to a nice sauce consistency, then pour over steaks and serve.

# GOAT CHEESE AND PINE NUT–CRUSTED BEEF TENDERLOIN

This is a classic way to combine the robust flavor of beef with the creaminess and earthy nature of goat cheese. It's a match made in heaven. **Serves 1**

2 tablespoons pine nuts

1 teaspoon chopped thyme

1 teaspoon chopped chives

½ clove garlic, minced

4 tablespoons fresh Texas goat
   cheese

2 pinches of kosher salt, divided

1 (7-ounce) beef tenderloin fillet

Pinch of freshly ground black pepper

½ teaspoon canola oil

Lightly toast the pine nuts in a dry nonstick pan to a light golden brown. Combine the herbs, garlic, goat cheese, and a pinch of salt. Season the fillet with salt and pepper, then sear in canola oil. Be sure to brown each side of the fillet before turning over to really caramelize the outside. If the beef is thick, it may be necessary to finish cooking in the oven. Cook to desired temperature. When the beef is almost finished, smother the top with the herb goat cheese mixture and place in the oven for 1 minute to warm the cheese. Top with the toasted pine nuts and serve.

# BEEF TENDERLOIN TOWER
# WITH CILANTRO PESTO

Here is a great dish for anyone trying to cut carbs. The ingredients are reasonably simple, but the flavors are bold.
**Serves 1** *(photo on page 137)*

---

Pesto
2 tablespoons pine nuts
1 bunch fresh basil, leaves only
1 bunch fresh cilantro, leaves only
1 tablespoon grated Parmesan
    cheese
1 anchovy fillet
1 small clove garlic
Juice of 1 lemon
1/2 teaspoon salt
1/2 cup plus 2 tablespoons extra
    virgin olive oil

Tower
3 (2-ounce) beef tenderloin
    medallions
2 pinches of kosher salt
Pinch of freshly ground black pepper
1 1/2 teaspoons olive oil
3 thick slices ripe tomato
2 slices fresh mozzarella
4–5 fresh cilantro sprigs

**Cilantro Pesto**
Lightly toast the pine nuts in a nonstick pan over medium heat until just lightly browned on all sides. Place all ingredients into a blender except the olive oil. While blending, slowly drizzle in the olive oil until a thick sauce consistency is achieved. Adjust the thickness of the pesto by adding or subtracting different amounts of oil if desired.

**Beef Tenderloin Tower**
Season the tenderloin on both sides with salt and pepper, then brown on both sides in olive oil. Remove from pan and then sear the tomato slices in the same pan. Stack the mozzarella, tomatoes, and beef alternately, ending with mozzarella on top. Put the stack under the broiler to brown the cheese, or lightly use a blowtorch to melt and brown the cheese on top just before serving. Drizzle the cilantro pesto over the plate and garnish with sprigs of cilantro.

---

# GRASS-FED TEXAS RIB-EYE WITH THREE-PEPPER COMPOUND BUTTER

I use beef raised by Jon and Wendy Taggart in Grandview, Texas, called Burgundy Pasture Beef. They produce the finest quality of beef I've ever tasted. They use no injections and no feed, and they follow completely sustainable agricultural practices. **Serves 1**

**Butter**
1 pound whole butter
¼ teaspoon kosher salt
1 fresh jalapeño pepper, finely diced
½ teaspoon ground chipotle powder
⅛ teaspoon chiles de arbol powder
¼ teaspoon cracked black pepper
2 cloves garlic, minced

**Rib-Eye**
1 (18-ounce) bone-in rib-eye steak
Pinch of kosher salt and freshly
   ground black pepper
1 teaspoon canola oil

**Three-Pepper Compound Butter**
Remove the butter from the fridge for about 30 minutes and allow it to soften almost to room temperature. Place in an electric mixer with the paddle attachment. Add all ingredients and blend well. Scrape down the sides of the bowl several times to make sure all ingredients are equally distributed. Pour the soft butter contents onto a sheet of parchment paper (or heavy plastic wrap) and roll into a 2- to 3-inch log shape. Refrigerate until ready to use. This butter will also freeze very well.

**Grass-Fed Texas Rib-Eye**
Season the steak with salt and pepper on both sides, then brush lightly with canola oil on both sides. Grill over pecan wood to desired temperature (I recommend 130 degrees F for medium-rare, about 6 to 8 minutes). Remove the steak from the grill and allow to rest for 2 to 3 minutes before cutting into it. While the steak is still hot, cut a slice of Three-Pepper Compound Butter and place right on top, allowing the butter to melt all over the steak and plate and then serve.

# MESQUITE-SMOKED, CHILE-RUBBED ROTISSERIE PRIME RIB

There are very few cooking techniques that can compete with the rotisserie for creating the juiciest meats possible, especially when cooking large cuts. This is a great dish to serve family style and carve right at the table for everyone to watch and enjoy. The spice blend and smoke really penetrate the beef in this preparation to create one of the most flavorful beef dishes imaginable. **Serves 10 to 12**

1 (12–15-pound) whole boneless
   rib-eye steak
2 cups Bonnell's Creole Seasoning
   Blend (page 182)

Clean the prime rib thoroughly. Pat dry and then rub well on all sides with the seasoning. Allow the rub to soak into the meat for at least 1$\frac{1}{2}$ hours. Place the prime rib on an electric rotisserie on medium heat. Add mesquite wood chips to the smoker box or, if your grill doesn't have one, place mesquite chips in aluminum foil and place over one burner on low to create a smoky environment. Be sure to cook with the lid closed to keep the smoke in, and replace the chips with fresh ones anytime the smoke dies down. Cook to an internal temperature of 130 to 135 degrees F and then remove. This should take approximately 1 to 1$\frac{1}{2}$ hours, but times can vary depending on the heat from different rotisseries, so be sure to check the internal temperature often. Allow the meat to rest for at least 20 minutes before cutting.

# SIRLOIN SUMMER STEAK TOPPED WITH SEARED AVOCADO AND SMOKY SALSA

I love the combination of different textures and temperatures in this dish. Cool crisp salsa with rich intensely flavored beef and creamy seared avocado makes for an extremely complex flavor profile for this dish. **Serves 2**

Salsa
1 ripe beefsteak tomato
1 ripe yellow tomato
2 poblano peppers
1 small purple onion
Juice of 2 limes
1 ear fresh sweet corn
1 tablespoon extra virgin olive oil
1/4 teaspoon hot smoked paprika
Pinch of kosher salt and freshly
    ground black pepper

Avocado
1 large ripe Hass avocado
Pinch of salt and pepper
1 teaspoon canola oil

Steak
2 (12–14-ounce) prime top
    sirloin steaks
1 teaspoon Bonnell's Creole
    Seasoning Blend (page 182)

**Smoky Salsa**

Remove the core from the red and yellow tomatoes and then place face up on a smoker rack. Allow to smoke over pecan wood for 10 to 15 minutes. Roast the poblano peppers over a grill or gas burner until blackened on all sides. Allow the peppers to sweat in a ziplock bag for 10 to 15 minutes and then remove the skins and seeds. Finely dice the peppers, tomatoes, and onion, and place in a mixing bowl with the lime juice. Allow to soak for at least 30 minutes (to tame the heat of the onion a bit). Roast a fresh ear of corn over an open grill until the kernels are lightly brown on all sides. Cut the corn from the cob and add to the salsa. Add the olive oil and paprika, and season with salt and pepper to taste just prior to serving (adding the salt too early will cause the salsa to lose its juices and become soupy).

**Seared Avocado**

Cut the avocado in half, remove the pit, and then remove avocado from the skin with a large spoon. Cut a small flat side on the bottom of the avocado to give a second flat surface that can be seared. Season with salt and pepper and then sear in a very hot medium-size nonstick pan with just a touch of oil until golden brown on both sides. This will develop a wonderfully complex, rich flavor for the avocado.

**Sirloin Summer Steak**

Rub the steaks well with the seasoning on all sides and allow to sit for 5 to 10 minutes before cooking. Grill to desired doneness (I recommend pulling the steaks at 130 degrees F). Allow the steak to rest after cooking for a few minutes prior to serving. Top with the seared avocado and a heaping mound of the smoked tomato and roasted corn salsa over the top and around the plate.

# SMOKED PORK CHOPS WITH JACK DANIEL'S AND GRANNY SMITH APPLE CIDER REDUCTION SAUCE

Pork has such a natural ability to absorb other flavors that smoking it just for a little while imparts a great smoky flavor that remains even after grilling it afterward. Apples and the sweet flavors of whiskey really bring out all of the best that pork has to offer. **Serves 4 large portions**

---

**Pork Chops**
1 whole frenched pork rack
    (usually 8 bones)
2 tablespoons Bonnell's Creole
    Seasoning Blend (page 182)

**Sauce**
1 small sweet onion, chopped
2 cloves garlic, minced
2 tablespoons butter
2 Granny Smith apples, peeled and
    diced into small cubes
1/2 teaspoon kosher salt
Pinch of ground black pepper
4 tablespoons Jack Daniel's
1 cup apple cider
1/2 cup chicken stock
2 tablespoons veal demiglace

**Smoked Pork Chops**
Season the rack of pork with seasoning and smoke at 120 degrees F for about 1 hour in a pecan wood smoker. This will not cook the pork but will give it a great smoky flavor. After the rack comes off the smoker, cut into individual chops and grill to desired doneness, dusting each side with a pinch more of seasoning.

**Jack Daniel's and Granny Smith Apple Cider Reduction Sauce**
In a medium saucepan, sauté the onion and garlic in butter. Add the apples after the onion has started to soften. Season with salt and pepper. Add the Jack Daniel's and flame. When the flame goes out, add the cider, stock, and demiglace. Reduce until slightly thick and then pour over the chops and serve.

---

# SMOKED PORK LOIN SANDWICH WITH SUN-DRIED TOMATO CREAM SAUCE

This sandwich, though one of the messiest, is one of the most flavorful ways to prepare pork. The complexity of smoke flavor combined with sweet and tart sun-dried tomatoes really works well with a rich, creamy sauce to hold all of these flavors together. **Serves 6**

Sauce
1 small onion
½ pound sun-dried tomatoes
2 cloves garlic, chopped
1 chipotle pepper (if using the canned type, rinse and remove seeds)
1½ teaspoons canola oil
Splash of dry white wine
2 cups cream
Pinch of kosher salt and freshly ground black pepper

Sandwich
2 pounds boneless pork loin
3 tablespoons Bonnell's Creole Seasoning Blend (page 182)
6 toasted rolls
1 purple onion, sliced very thinly

**Sun-Dried Tomato Sauce**
In a medium saucepan, sauté the onion, tomatoes, garlic, and chipotle in canola oil until the onion becomes soft. Deglaze the pan with wine and then add the cream. Bring to a light simmer for 5 minutes, then purée with a stick blender until very smooth. Season with salt and pepper, and reduce until the sauce becomes slightly thick.

**Smoked Pork Loin Sandwich**
Rub all sides of the pork loin in seasoning and allow to sit for 2 to 3 hours. Smoke with pecan wood to an internal temperature of 140 degrees F. Remove from the smoker, wrap with plastic, and refrigerate. When cool, slice very thin and simmer each portion in Sun-Dried Tomato Sauce for about 30 seconds to 1 minute before serving. After coating the meat in the sauce, place slices on a toasted roll, and top with onion.

★ ★ ★

# SIDE DISHES

★ Cast-Iron Sweet Cornbread ★
★ Chile Relleno with Cilantro Pesto and Goat Cheese ★
★ Creamy Grits with Shrimp ★
★ Truffled Shoestring Potatoes ★
★ Fresh Herb and Goat Cheese–Stuffed Portobellos ★
★ Grilled Polenta ★
★ Herb-Roasted Fingerling Potatoes ★
★ Jalapeño Parmesan Creamed Spinach ★
★ Crispy 1015 Tobacco Onions ★
★ Manchego and Sage Grits ★
★ Roasted Green Chile Cheese Grits ★
★ Roasted Jalapeño Twice-Baked Potatoes ★
★ Sherry-Laced Mushrooms ★
★ Bonnell's Southwestern Seasoning Blend ★
★ Bonnell's Creole Seasoning Blend ★

As impressive as a steak can be, the meal just isn't complete without a little something on the side. A perfectly executed steak with rich sauce clinging to every bite can be elevated by the crispy sweet nature of perfectly fried tobacco onion rings or by deliciously seasoned roasted potatoes. The Texas table just seems barren without some contrast, even if the star of the show is magnificent. Thanksgiving wouldn't be the same if the turkey sat on the table all alone. The sides play the supporting role for most dishes, but it's an important role nonetheless. Of all the dishes I've ever created—all the sauces, all the dressings and marinades—one recipe stands out as the most requested by far: the green chile cheese grits. Everyone just has to know how I make the grits. Even on a mixed grill entrée loaded with homemade Andouille sausage, axis venison, elk, and a wild-game demiglace (that takes three days to make) everyone, without exception, asks for the recipe for the grits. Everyone comes for the meats, but they come back for the sides. ★

*Creamy Grits with Shrimp, recipe on page 162.*

# CAST-IRON SWEET CORNBREAD

This sweet cornbread almost seems more like a dessert than a bread. It pairs perfectly with heavy soups like gumbo or chili to warm the soul on a cold day. Cast-iron cooking is the key to browning the cornbread evenly on all sides.
**Serves 4 to 6**

---

3/4 cup bread flour
1/2 cup cornmeal
4 tablespoons sugar
1 tablespoon powdered milk
1 tablespoon baking powder
1/2 teaspoon salt
2 eggs
2/3 cup milk
1/3 cup vegetable oil
1/4 teaspoon vanilla extract
1/4 cup kernel corn (frozen
    works fine)
Nonstick spray

**Large Batch Option**
3 cups bread flour
1 1/4 cups cornmeal
1 cup + 2 tablespoons sugar
1/4 cup powdered milk
4 tablespoons baking powder
1 tablespoon salt

Mix all dry ingredients in a bowl with a whisk. Mix all wet ingredients separately, then combine with dry (make sure the eggs are mixed well) to form a uniform batter.

Preheat 6-inch cast-iron pans to 375 degrees F in convection oven. Pull the pans out while hot, spray well with nonstick spray, and add batter to each pan (no more than half full). Bake approximately 7 to 8 minutes until golden brown on top. To test for doneness, poke a toothpick through the middle. If it comes out dry, the cornbread is done. This can be done in a large cast-iron pan or smaller individual pans, but the cooking times may vary slightly. Using preheated cast iron makes all the difference in this cornbread by allowing all sides to brown at the same time.

**Large Batch Option**
Mix a large batch of the dry ingredients ahead of time, then add the perishable liquid ingredients as needed for each batch. This will make approximately 4 batches.

Mix all dry ingredients with a whisk and then store together in a ziplock bag. When ready to make a batch, mix 1 2/3 cups dry ingredients with the same wet ingredients as in the original recipe and follow the same directions.

---

# CHILE RELLENO WITH CILANTRO PESTO AND GOAT CHEESE

Although actually a vegetarian dish, this chile relleno has a heavy stick-to-your-ribs kind of quality that can work well as a complete dish or as a side item. **Serves 1**

1 large poblano pepper
1 small red bell pepper
¼ cup chopped yellow squash
¼ cup chopped zucchini
¼ cup chopped eggplant
2 cloves garlic, chopped
½ small onion, chopped
1½ teaspoons olive oil
Pinch of kosher salt
2 tablespoons Cilantro Pesto
   (page 145)
3 tablespoons fresh goat cheese
4 tablespoons grated
   Monterey Jack cheese
Creole Sauce (page 88)

Roast the poblano and bell pepper until charred on the outside. Place in a ziplock bag, allow to sweat for about 10 minutes, and remove from bag. Remove the skins with the back of a knife. For the poblano pepper, carefully cut a small slit down one side and remove the seeds while keeping the pepper whole, it will be stuffed later. For the bell pepper, remove the seeds and slice into strips. In a large skillet, sauté the remaining vegetables in olive oil until the ingredients are tender; season with salt. Stuff the poblano with the vegetable mixture and then top with pesto, and cheeses. Bake until the ingredients are hot and the cheese is melted. Serve with Creole Sauce over rice.

# CREAMY GRITS WITH SHRIMP

This is a Southern classic made with Texas shrimp. Always look for wild-caught Texas shrimp or Texas farm-raised shrimp, but avoid cheaper varieties from other countries. **Serves 4 to 6**

## Grits
1/2 cup chopped onion
1 teaspoon chopped garlic
1 teaspoon butter
2 teaspoons Frank's RedHot Sauce
1 cup heavy cream
1 cup chicken stock
2 tablespoons Bonnell's Creole
    Seasoning Blend (page 182)
1/2 cup Homestead Gristmill Grits
1/2 cup plus 2 tablespoons grated
    Monterey Jack cheese

## Shrimp
2 links hot Andouille sausage
1 teaspoon butter
12–14 large (16–20 count) shrimp,
    peeled and deveined
1/2 cup heavy cream
1 teaspoon Frank's RedHot Sauce
Salt and pepper, to taste

## Creamy Grits
Sauté the onion and garlic in butter until soft. Add hot sauce, cream, and stock, and bring to a simmer (the stage just before a rolling boil). Be careful not to let the liquids boil over. Quickly whisk in seasoning and grits while simmering. Stir constantly until grits begin to thicken; simmer 15 to 20 minutes. Turn down to low. Gently fold in cheese and let sit for at least 5 minutes.

## Shrimp
Dice the sausage into small cubes, then sauté in butter until slightly browned. Add the shrimp and cook over medium heat for 1 minute. Add cream and hot sauce, and reduce until thick. Season with salt and pepper, and then pour the entire pan over the grits.

# TRUFFLED SHOESTRING POTATOES

Common as they are, French fries are actually quite tricky to pull off. This recipe combines the crispy texture of thinly sliced potatoes with a luxurious nature of truffles. **Serves 3 to 4**

2 large baking potatoes

1 cup buttermilk

2 cups flour

2 teaspoons iodized salt, plus more to taste

¼ teaspoon freshly ground black pepper

3 quarts canola oil

¼ teaspoon white winter truffle oil

Cut the potatoes into long thin julienne strips (peeling is optional). Soak in buttermilk for at least 20 minutes. Pull out a handful of the potatoes at a time and dredge in a mixture of flour, salt, and pepper until well coated on all sides. Deep-fry at 375 degrees F until lightly golden brown, turning over frequently to ensure that they fry evenly on all sides. Drain on paper towels as soon as they come out of the fryer and lightly season with just a pinch of salt. Drizzle each portion while hot with a few drops of white truffle oil just before serving.

# FRESH HERB AND GOAT CHEESE-STUFFED PORTOBELLOS

This is a great dish to cook on the grill as an alternative to just meats. It's technically vegetarian, but it is as rich and bold in flavor as any steak. **Serves 3**

---

3 large portobello mushrooms
2 teaspoons extra virgin olive oil
Pinch of kosher salt, plus more to taste
1 cup crumbled fresh goat cheese (I recommend Deborah Rogers Farmstead Cheese)
1 small clove garlic, minced
Pepper, to taste
2 fresh thyme sprigs
1 fresh cilantro sprig
1 fresh rosemary sprig
1 fresh dill sprig
2 large fresh basil leaves

Clean the dark black gills from the mushrooms, then drizzle with a little olive oil, season with salt, and place face down over medium heat on an open barbecue grill. After a few minutes, turn them over and continue to cook. In a small mixing bowl, combine the goat cheese with garlic, salt, pepper, and fresh herbs torn by hand. Mix the cheese until all of the ingredients have been incorporated and a nice creamy texture is achieved. When the mushrooms begin to soften and give off a little of their juice, place a nice spoonful of the cheese mixture into the center of each. Close the lid of the barbecue and let cook until the cheese gets bubbly and the mushrooms are nice and soft.

---

# GRILLED POLENTA

Polenta is usually served soft and warm, but this recipe takes polenta one step further. I love the complexity and richness that grilling the polenta adds. **Serves 10**

---

2 cups milk
2 tablespoons butter
2 cups chicken stock
1 cup polenta or cornmeal
1 teaspoon salt
¼ teaspoon cracked black pepper
¼ cup grated Parmesan cheese

Bring milk, butter, and stock to a simmer. Whisk in the polenta, salt, and pepper, and cook on low, stirring constantly, until the polenta has absorbed all of the liquid. Once the polenta begins to thicken, add the cheese. Pour the contents into a 10 x 14-inch baking dish lined with parchment paper (the paper isn't necessary if it's a nonstick surface). Refrigerate overnight and allow to set up. Remove the polenta from the pan, and using a cookie cutter, cut into bars, triangles, or any shape you prefer. Spray a light even coat of nonstick spray on each piece and grill over high heat until nice grill marks appear, then turn over and repeat. Be sure to spray each side with the nonstick spray or the polenta will stick. Once the polenta has grilled on both sides and is warm throughout, it's ready to serve.

---

# HERB-ROASTED FINGERLING POTATOES

These flavorful little potatoes make the perfect accompaniment for any steak or chop. They can even be served chilled for a picnic. **Serves 8**

3 pounds fingerling potatoes
1 red bell pepper, diced into
    medium cubes
1 poblano pepper, diced into
    medium cubes
1 Texas 1015 sweet onion,
    diced into large cubes
2 teaspoons dried basil
1 teaspoon dried thyme
1 teaspoon kosher salt
¼ teaspoon freshly ground
    black pepper
4 tablespoons olive oil
1 tablespoon Worcestershire sauce
Juice of 1 lemon

Cut the fingerlings into halves and toss well in a large mixing bowl with all other ingredients. Pour the contents into a large roasting pan and roast in a 400-degree F convection oven, stirring the mixture every 15 minutes, until the potatoes are soft and golden brown on the outside. This should take approximately 40 minutes, but the time may vary depending on the size of the potato pieces and the type of oven.

# JALAPEÑO PARMESAN CREAMED SPINACH

This creamed spinach with jalapeños has just enough spice to keep it interesting, but not enough to hurt anyone.
**Serves 3 to 4**

2 jalapeños, seeded and chopped
1 clove garlic, chopped
1 teaspoon olive oil
1 pound baby spinach, washed
1 cup cream
½ teaspoon kosher salt
¼ cup grated Parmesan cheese

Sauté the jalapeños and garlic in olive oil until the garlic begins to sizzle. Do not let it brown or the dish will take on a bitter flavor. Add the baby spinach to the pan in one large heap. As it begins to wilt, add the cream and turn the spinach often. As soon as the cream begins to simmer, the spinach will wilt quickly. As it wilts, season with salt and add the cheese. Once the spinach is fully wilted, it's ready to serve.

# CRISPY 1015 TOBACCO ONIONS

The Texas 1015 is an exceptionally sweet yellow onion that was developed by Texas A&M University. The name 1015 comes from the date they are planted, October 15, which also happens to be my birthday. They tend to be one of the first onions available in the spring, and they can easily reach the size of a softball. **Serves 6 to 8**

1 cup buttermilk
3 tablespoons Crystal Hot Sauce
1 large Texas 1015 onion
1 cup flour
1 tablespoon Bonnell's Creole
   Seasoning Blend (page 182)

Combine the buttermilk and hot sauce. Cut the onion into thin rings and soak in buttermilk mixture for at least 2 hours. Combine the flour and seasoning in a mixing bowl. Pull the rings out of the buttermilk mixture and dredge in the seasoned flour until well coated. Fry at 350 degrees F until golden brown and crispy on all sides. Drain on paper towels.

# MANCHEGO AND SAGE GRITS

I've never met grits that I didn't like. All it takes to make grits taste good is a flavorful liquid for them to absorb. Water has no flavor at all, so I almost never cook with it. Grits are just waiting for something delicious to soak up and are more than willing to carry plenty of other flavors. **Serves 4**

½ cup chopped onion
1 teaspoon chopped garlic
1 teaspoon butter
½ teaspoon kosher salt
¼ teaspoon freshly ground black
 pepper
1 cup chicken stock
1 cup heavy cream
½ cup Homestead Gristmill Grits
2 tablespoons chopped fresh sage
½ cup plus 2 tablespoons grated
 manchego cheese

Sweat the onion and garlic in butter until the onion becomes soft. Add salt, pepper, stock, and cream, and bring to a light simmer. Whisk in the grits and sage vigorously to the simmering liquid and turn the heat to low. Continue stirring until the grits soak up the liquid. This can be done in 5 minutes if using instant grits, or it may take 15 to 20 minutes for stone-ground grits. Once the grits are cooked and have absorbed most of the liquid, fold in the cheese and serve.

# ROASTED GREEN CHILE CHEESE GRITS

I had trouble convincing people in other parts of the country that grits could be on a fine dining menu, but in Fort Worth it's my most requested recipe by far. Anyone who's ever tasted these grits ends up wondering why anyone would just cook grits in water to begin with. **Serves 6**

1 fresh poblano pepper
1/2 cup chopped sweet onion
1 teaspoon chopped garlic
1 teaspoon butter
1 cup chicken stock
1 cup heavy cream
1/2 teaspoon kosher salt
1/4 teaspoon ground black pepper
1/2 cup Homestead Gristmill Grits
4 tablespoons grated
    cheddar cheese
4 tablespoons grated Monterey
    Jack cheese
Pico de Gallo (page 16)

Roast the poblano over an open fire until black on all sides. (This can be done over a grill or over a gas burner. If you have a kitchen without gas, place the poblano on the top rack under the broiler in your oven.) Once the pepper is black on all sides, place in a ziplock bag and allow to sweat for 10–15 minutes, or until cool enough to handle. Using the back side of a knife blade, scrape off the black outer skin, then slice open and remove the seeds, veins, and stem. Finely dice the chile and then sauté in a saucepan with the onion and garlic in butter. Once the onion becomes soft, add the stock and cream, and bring to a simmer. Season with salt and pepper as it simmers and vigorously whisk in the grits. Turn the heat to low and continue to whisk the grits until they have absorbed most of the liquid. Fold in the cheeses and stir until incorporated. The grits will take anywhere from 5 to 20 minutes to cook, depending on the type of grits used. Instant grits easily cook in 5 minutes, but stone-ground grits can take up to 20 minutes to soften. Garnish with Pico de Gallo.

# ROASTED JALAPEÑO
# TWICE-BAKED POTATOES

These versatile little potatoes make a great passed appetizer, buffet item, or entrée plate presentation. **Serves 6 to 8**

3 pounds small new potatoes

3 tablespoons butter

1/2 cup sour cream

1 teaspoon salt

1/2 teaspoon freshly ground
   black pepper

2 fresh jalapeño peppers, plus
   thin slices for garnish

3 scallions (green parts only),
   chopped

1/2 cup grated cheddar cheese

3 strips bacon, cooked

Boil the potatoes until slightly soft. (The amount of time will depend on what type of potatoes you decide to buy. I like baby reds for this dish, which generally can be boiled in approximately 15 minutes.) Remove potatoes from the boiling water and chill. Cut into halves and scoop out as much of the inner potato as possible, while still leaving enough of the skin to stay together. In a small saucepan, warm the butter, sour cream, salt, and pepper, and then pour the contents over the potato. Roast the jalapeños until black on all sides, then place in a ziplock bag and allow to sweat for 10 minutes. Scrape off the black skins with the back edge of a knife blade and remove the seeds and stem. Chop the jalapeños and combine with the potatoes; add the scallions. Mix well and then stuff the mixture back into the potato skins. Top each with grated cheese and pieces of bacon, and bake in the oven at 325 degrees F until warmed through, about 8 to 10 minutes. For an extra garnish, top with thinly shaved slices of fresh jalapeño. The amount of jalapeño can be altered, depending on the tolerance of your crowd.

# SHERRY-LACED MUSHROOMS

Wild mushrooms are perfect for fall and winter recipes. I love how the sweetness of sherry balances out the earthy flavor of the mushrooms. **Serves 6** *(photo on page 133)*

1 shallot, minced

2 cloves garlic, chopped

3 cups assorted roughly cut wild mushrooms (crimini, oyster, hen of the woods, shiitake, chanterelle, and morel are best for this dish, but any combination will work)

1 teaspoon canola oil

¼ teaspoon dried lavender

6 tablespoons dry cream sherry

3 tablespoons heavy cream

1 tablespoon veal demiglace

3 fresh thyme sprigs

Pinch of kosher salt and freshly ground black pepper

In a saucepan, sauté the shallot, garlic, and mushrooms in canola oil until the mushrooms begin to soften. Add the lavender and then the sherry to the pan and allow it to flame off. Once the sherry has reduced by just over half, add the cream, demiglace, and thyme. Season with salt and pepper; once the sauce has reduced to a thick coating consistency, it's ready to serve.

# BONNELL'S SOUTHWESTERN SEASONING BLEND

★  ★  ★

This is my favorite seasoning blend to use on steaks or chops cooked over a wood-burning grill. It blends a little Mexican flavor with a complex Southwestern backbone.

**5 tablespoons iodized salt**
**2 tablespoons granulated garlic**
**2 tablespoons fine black pepper**
**2 teaspoons cayenne pepper**
**3/4 tablespoon dried thyme**
**3/4 tablespoon dried oregano**
**2 tablespoons paprika**
**1 tablespoon onion powder**
**1/2 tablespoon dried basil**
**1/2 tablespoon cumin**
**2 teaspoons coriander**
**2 tablespoons chili powder**
**1/2 tablespoon dry mustard powder**

Toss all ingredients together in a bowl and store in an airtight container.

# BONNELL'S CREOLE SEASONING BLEND

Every chef who uses a Creole blend tends to mix theirs a bit differently. I think this combination has just the right amount of spice and complexity, without being too exotic. I use this blend as an all-purpose seasoning on everything from fish to game. It's extremely versatile.

---

10 tablespoons iodized salt
4 tablespoons granulated garlic
4 tablespoons fine black pepper
1 tablespoon cayenne
1½ tablespoons dried thyme
1½ tablespoons dried oregano
5¾ tablespoons paprika
2 tablespoons onion powder
1 tablespoon dried basil

Toss all ingredients together in a bowl and store in an airtight container.

---

# DESSERTS AND BEVERAGES

★ Banana-Pecan Crêpes with Caramel Sauce ★

★ Black-and-White Chocolate Mousse ★

★ Blackberry Empanadas with Huckleberry Cream ★

★ Blueberry and Peach Beggar's Purse with Orange and Ginger Sauce ★

★ Caramel Pecan Cheesecake with Caramel Sauce ★

★ Caramelized Banana Sundae ★

★ Cast-Iron Cinnamon Apple Crisp ★

★ Fresh Berry Cobbler with Sweet Biscuit Dough ★

★ Margarita Cheesecake ★

★ Tres Leches Crème Brûlée ★

★ Dublin Dr. Pepper Float with Cinnamon Bunuelo Cookies ★

★ Bonnell's Chocolate Chip Cookie Martini ★

★ Bonnell's Brandy Ice ★

★ Mint Chocolate Chip Smoothie ★

★ Smokehouse Cocktail ★

★ Texas Sunset ★

★ Ultimate Cowtown Cosmo ★

★ White Chocolate Martini ★

These are the perfect bookends to a great meal. Start off the night with a stellar cocktail, and finish the evening with a little something sweet. In many cases, a sweet cocktail can even replace the dessert course altogether when there isn't enough room for a full serving. Texas desserts often try to straddle that fine line between comfort food and fancy fare. Few Texans feel comfortable tearing into a gravity-defying tower, even if it may be a masterpiece of pastry excellence. Then again, just a plain scoop of pudding in a bowl doesn't quite cut it here either. The balance lies somewhere in the middle, where it takes a homemade touch and some real skill to pull it off, but falls short of pretentious. Texas desserts tend to be approachable, usually straightforward, and always straight from the heart. ★

*Black-and-White Chocolate Mousse, recipe on page 188.*

# BANANA-PECAN CRÊPES WITH CARAMEL SAUCE

These crepes take a bit of effort to prepare, but the results are worth it. The rich, creamy texture of the pastry cream pairs perfectly with the texture of crisp pecans. **Serves 4 to 6**

---

**Caramel Sauce**
3 tablespoons water
1 cup sugar
1 cup heavy cream

**Crêpes**
2 tablespoons melted butter, plus ½ teaspoon butter for the crêpe pan
1 cup all-purpose flour
Pinch of kosher salt
3 large eggs, lightly beaten
1¼ cups milk

**Pastry Cream**
1 cup whole milk
1 cup heavy cream
½ teaspoon cinnamon
5 large egg yolks
½ cup sugar
4 tablespoons cornstarch
2 tablespoons unsalted butter
1 teaspoon vanilla extract
¼ cup white chocolate morsels
¼ cup chopped pecans
2 bananas, sliced

**Caramel Sauce**

In a very clean saucepan (do not use nonstick) over medium-high heat, add water and sugar. Stir and watch carefully until sugar melts and turns a golden brown. (Keep a watchful eye on sugar because it can go from golden brown to burned beyond recognition in about 1 minute.)

Immediately remove from heat and whisk in cream slowly, adding just a little cream at first and stirring the rest in gradually. Stir constantly until smooth. At this point, caramel sauce will be very thin. After it cools, it will thicken. Be very cautious when adding cream to sugar, as the pan will start to violently bubble.

**Crêpes**

Preheat a crêpe pan and melt ½ teaspoon butter in the bottom. Mix all ingredients well (a stick blender works great for this). Pour just enough batter to cover the bottom of the pan with a thin layer. When crêpe is brown, carefully flip over and brown the other side. Put the cooked crêpe on a plate and place a square of wax paper on top to keep from sticking to the next crêpe. Alternate crêpes and paper until the batter is used up.

**Pastry Cream**

Combine all ingredients except pecans and banana in a small saucepan and gently bring to a boil while whisking thoroughly. When the mixture boils, turn heat to low. Boil for 1 minute and then cool. Place in a bowl and cover with plastic wrap to avoid a skin forming on the surface. Fill each crêpe with Pastry Cream, pecans, and bananas, and roll up like an enchilada. Serve topped with Caramel Sauce and more pecans and banana pieces.

---

★ **OPTIONAL:** This dish also works well with a topping of Bourbon-Spiked Whipped Cream.

**Bourbon-Spiked Whipped Cream**
Combine 1 cup heavy cream, 2 tablespoons bourbon, 1 teaspoon sugar, and ½ teaspoon cinnamon; whip until stiff peaks form.

# BLACK-AND-WHITE CHOCOLATE MOUSSE

I love the combination of dark chocolate and white chocolate next to each other on the plate. Serving a little liqueur with this dish is just an added bonus for special occasions. **Serves 8 to 10**

---

**Black Chocolate Mousse**
5 eggs, separated
1 pint heavy whipping cream
1 tablespoon sugar, divided
10 ounces semisweet dark chocolate
3 tablespoons shortening

**White Chocolate Mousse**
5 eggs, separated
1 pint heavy whipping cream
1 tablespoon sugar, divided
10 ounces white chocolate
3 tablespoons shortening

**Black Chocolate Mousse**
Whip egg whites to a stiff peak. Whip the cream in a mixer with 1 teaspoon sugar. Melt the chocolate and shortening together gently in a large mixing bowl over a double boiler. Remove from heat. In a separate small bowl, mix remaining sugar with the egg yolks. After chocolate is completely melted, whisk the yolk mixture in thoroughly. Gently fold the whipped egg whites into the chocolate mixture, being careful not to deflate the egg whites completely. Finally, fold in the whipped cream. Refrigerate at least 1 hour. Can be refrigerated for 2 days. Serve chilled.

**White Chocolate Mousse**
Follow directions for Black Chocolate Mousse. The white chocolate mousse will have a thinner consistency. Serve both together and sprinkle the top with chocolate shavings.

---

★ **OPTIONAL:** I like to garnish this dish with a little shooter of chocolate and raspberry liqueur for fun. I mix equal parts of Godiva dark chocolate liqueur with Chambord.

# BLACKBERRY EMPANADAS WITH HUCKLEBERRY CREAM

These little fried pies are the perfect celebration of summer, when the blackberries are plentiful and sweet. Huckleberries make a great sauce for these little pastries with just the right amount of tartness for balance. **Serves 10 to 12**

---

**Huckleberry Cream**
1 pound fresh or frozen huckleberries
1/3 cup sugar
1 pint heavy whipping cream
1/4 cup Grand Marnier

**Blackberry Filling**
3 pints fresh blackberries, divided
1/4 cup granulated sugar
2 tablespoons dark rum
2 teaspoons cornstarch

**Empanada Dough**
1/2 cup sugar
2 tablespoons vegetable shortening
1 egg
1/2 cup milk
2 cups all-purpose flour
1 teaspoon baking powder
1/2 teaspoon salt
1 pint blackberries
2 quarts canola oil
1/4 cup confectioners' sugar

**Huckleberry Cream**
Combine all ingredients in a saucepan and simmer for 8 to 10 minutes. Purée with a stick blender and chill.

**Blackberry Filling**
In a saucepan, cook 2½ pints blackberries with sugar, rum, and cornstarch until the juices have all been released and the sauce begins to thicken. Reserve the remaining whole berries for stuffing into the empanadas whole. Strain out the seeds and cool the mixture.

**Empanada Dough**
Place all ingredients except blackberries, canola oil, and confectioners' sugar into a large mixing bowl and combine gently by hand just until the dough is a consistent, uniform texture with no lumps. Liberally flour a smooth kitchen surface and roll out the dough to approximately 1/8 to 1/4 inch thick. Cut out circles with a round cookie cutter. Fill the center of each with a spoonful of the blackberry filling and 1 to 2 fresh berries. Fold over to form a half moon and use the tines of a fork to seal the edges. If the edges have trouble sealing, use a touch of beaten egg yolk as a binder. Refrigerate for 5 to 10 minutes before frying. Fry in oil at 350 degree F until the dough turns a light golden brown (approximately 1 minute). Remove from the oil and drain on paper towels. Serve with huckleberry cream and a generous sprinkling of confectioners' sugar.

---

★ **NOTE:** Huckleberry cream can be used as a sauce or whipped into a beautiful purple whipped cream once it's chilled.

# BLUEBERRY AND PEACH BEGGAR'S PURSE WITH ORANGE AND GINGER SAUCE

I created this particular dish to serve at The James Beard House in New York. It may take some labor to create, but it pairs perfectly with a late harvest dessert wine. **Serves 4**

---

### Sauce
2 cups milk
2 cups heavy cream
$1/4$ vanilla bean
$1/4$-inch piece fresh ginger
$1/2$ cup sugar, divided
8 eggs
12 oranges, segmented

### Crêpes
3 eggs
$1 1/4$ cups milk
2 tablespoons butter, melted
$1/2$ cup flour
$1/2$ teaspoon salt
Canola oil

### Beggar's Purse
2 fresh peaches, peeled and halved
1 tablespoon unsalted butter
2 tablespoons brown sugar
Pinch of cinnamon
1 tablespoon peach Schnapps
1 tablespoon dark rum
1 cup fresh blueberries

### Orange and Ginger Sauce
Heat the milk, cream, vanilla bean, and ginger with $1/4$ cup sugar in a medium saucepan. Bring to a light simmer and then turn off the heat. Combine the eggs with the other half of the sugar and whisk well in a large mixing bowl. Slowly add the hot cream mixture to the eggs while whisking vigorously; begin with just a few drops and slowly increase the rate of pouring as the mixture starts to come together. Place the entire mixture back into the saucepan and heat very gently, stirring the entire time. Watch very carefully at this point. As soon as the sauce begins to thicken at all, pull it from the heat and cool in an ice bath immediately. If it cooks too long, the eggs will curdle and must be discarded; then you have to start over. Once the sauce is thickening, strain the mixture to remove the ginger and vanilla bean, and add the orange segments.

### Crêpes
Combine all ingredients except canola oil until smooth; let batter rest about 1 hour. Heat a crêpe pan or small sauté pan over medium heat for 1 to 2 minutes and add just a drizzle of canola oil. Drop $1/4$ cup batter on pan and quickly tilt the pan to spread batter evenly over entire surface. Cook until the edges start to brown, then flip and cook other side until lightly browned. Remove and place on squares of wax paper until ready to use.

### Blueberry and Peach Beggar's Purse
In a nonstick medium-size pan, cook peaches in butter until soft, about 1 to 2 minutes, and then add sugar and cinnamon. When sugar is melted, add Schnapps and rum, and cook about 2 minutes more. Remove from the heat and allow to cool slightly. Fill each peach half with blueberries where the pit used to be, then wrap each peach with a crêpe. Pull the crêpe up and hold the edges together on top with several toothpicks to form a beggar's purse. Place each one on a greased baking sheet and bake for 12 minutes at 350 degrees F. Remove toothpicks and serve with the sauce.

---

★ **OPTIONAL:** Garnish the plate with orange wedges and blueberries.

# CARAMEL PECAN CHEESECAKE WITH CARAMEL SAUCE

Texas has long been known for its pecans. When they are fresh, we try to use them in every dish we can.
**Serves 10 to 12**

**Crust**
1 cup graham cracker crumbs
1 tablespoon sugar
1 teaspoon cinnamon

**Cheesecake**
1½ cups sugar
3 pounds plain cream cheese, softened
5 eggs
1 teaspoon vanilla extract
1 teaspoon gelatin powder
²/₃ cup Caramel Sauce (page 186)
²/₃ cup chopped pecans

**Crust**
Combine all ingredients and pat evenly across the bottom and slightly up the sides of a springform pan.

**Caramel Pecan Cheesecake**
In a large mixer, add the sugar and cream cheese, and mix with the paddle attachment for 2 minutes. Slowly add the eggs, one at a time, until completely incorporated. Add the vanilla and gelatin, and blend until the cake reaches a uniform consistency. Pour one-third of the cake batter into the springform pan over the crust. Drizzle with one-third of the Caramel Sauce and sprinkle in one-third of the pecans. Repeat the layering process and end with a layer of batter. Bake in a 275-degree F oven for approximately 3 hours, or until the middle has cooked through. Cool in the pan. To release the cheesecake from the sides of the pan, cut around the edge with a paring knife dipped in warm water. Run the knife around the sides several times, release the spring, and remove the cake from the pan. Serve with warmed Caramel Sauce.

# CARAMELIZED BANANA SUNDAE

A homemade ice cream is a rare treat these days. Nothing can make an occasion more special than a dish like this when everything is made from scratch. **Serves 1**

Sauce
3/4 cup half-and-half
4 tablespoons amaretto
1/4 teaspoon pure vanilla extract
1 tablespoon unsalted butter
1 1/3 cups semisweet chocolate chips

Sundae
1/2 banana
1/2 teaspoon granulated sugar
3 scoops premium vanilla ice cream
1 strawberry, chopped
2 teaspoons chopped pecans
3 tablespoons Chocolate Sauce
3 tablespoons Caramel Sauce
   (page 186)

**Chocolate Sauce**
Bring the half-and-half, amaretto, vanilla, and butter to a light simmer. Pour over the chocolate in a bowl, let sit for about 1 minute, and then whisk until smooth. If necessary, place back on gentle heat to warm, but never place over high heat. Serve warm when ready to use.

**Caramelized Banana Sundae**
Cut the banana in half lengthwise and sprinkle granulated sugar on the flat side. Caramelize sugar with a blowtorch until light golden brown. Place in a bowl or deep plate with ice cream and dress with all of the sundae toppings. I like to serve this in an edible cookie cup that's made by baking a cookie draped over an inverted bowl.

# CAST-IRON CINNAMON APPLE CRISP

This is my Texas version of apple pie. It works best when served sizzling in cast-iron straight from the oven. **Serves 6 (1 large pie)**

---

**Topping**
1 cup brown sugar
1 cup flour
1/2 cup sliced almonds
1/2 cup butter

**Apple Crisp**
9 Granny Smith apples
1/2 cup brown sugar
1/2 cup white sugar
Juice of 1 lime
2 teaspoons cinnamon, or to taste

**Topping**
In a Cuisinart-type food processor, blend together the brown sugar, flour, and almonds. When the mixture gets almost smooth, add chunks of the butter and pulse until the mixture becomes the consistency of wet sand. Do not overmix or the topping will become gluey.

**Cast-Iron Cinnamon Apple Crisp**
Peel the apples, slice and dust with both sugars, lime juice, and desired amount of cinnamon; allow to sit in a large mixing bowl for 10 minutes to marinate.

In a cast-iron skillet (any size will work!), preheat the pan to 300 degrees F in a convection oven. Grease the pan with just a touch of butter (or spray with nonstick spray), then add a 3- to 4-inch-thick layer of the apple mixture. Top with a 1-inch-thick layer of the crumbled topping and bake at 300 degrees F for approximately 60 minutes. Keep checking to be sure that the top does not get too brown. If this happens, lower the temperature to 275 degrees F and keep an eye on the pie. When the topping is golden brown and the apples are lightly bubbling, the dessert is ready. Serve in the pan family style, or scoop out and top with cinnamon ice cream.

---

# FRESH BERRY COBBLER WITH SWEET BISCUIT DOUGH

Cobblers are a staple in Texas when all kinds of berries are fresh. I love the simplicity of this dessert with warm berries and sweet biscuits to soak up all the sweet, syrupy goodness. **Serves 8 to 10**

---

Dough
2 cups flour
1/2 cup sugar
1/4 cup powdered milk
1 tablespoon baking powder
3/4 teaspoon salt
1/2 cup vegetable shortening
3/4 cup buttermilk

Cobbler
1 cup blackberries
1 cup blueberries
1 cup quartered strawberries
1/2 cup plus 6 tablespoons sugar, divided
2 tablespoons Grand Marnier
3 tablespoons dark rum
1/2 teaspoon cornstarch
Confectioners' sugar, for garnish

**Sweet Biscuit Dough**
Mix all dry ingredients together and sift. Cut in cubes of shortening by hand until it reaches the consistency of wet sand. Add cold buttermilk slowly, just until the dough starts to come together. Be sure not to overmix. Roll out to 1/4 inch thick, cut into circles, and place one circle on top of each cobbler.

**Fresh Berry Cobbler**
Combine all ingredients except confectioners' sugar in a mixing bowl, mix thoroughly without breaking up all of the berries, and then fill individual ramekins (like crème brûlée dishes) with the mixture. Top with a circle of the sweet biscuit dough and sprinkle a little sugar on top of the dough. Bake at 350 degrees F until the dough has risen and the berry mixture is hot and bubbly. This should take approximately 12 minutes, depending on the thickness of the dough and the size of the ramekins. Look for the biscuit to turn golden and be sure that it has risen before removing from the oven. Garnish with a light dusting of confectioners' sugar. Ice cream also makes a great topper for this dish!

---

# MARGARITA CHEESECAKE

Any time of year is a great time to enjoy cheesecake, but the summertime is the best time to enjoy the state drink of Texas in a dessert format. **Serves 10 to 12**

---

### Crust
1 cup graham cracker crumbs
1 tablespoon sugar
1 teaspoon cinnamon

### Cheesecake
1½ cups sugar
3 pounds plain cream cheese, softened
6 eggs
1 teaspoon vanilla extract
1 cup margarita mix
1 tablespoon grated lime zest
2 tablespoons lime juice
1 teaspoon gelatin powder
Lime zest, orange zest, or candied lime slices, for garnish

### Crust
Combine all ingredients and pat evenly across the bottom and slightly up the sides of a springform pan.

### Margarita Cheesecake
In a large mixer, add the sugar and cream cheese, and mix with the paddle attachment for 2 minutes. Slowly add the eggs, one at a time, until completely incorporated. Add remaining ingredients and blend until the cheesecake reaches a uniform consistency. Pour the batter into the springform pan over the crust, then bake in a 275-degree F oven for approximately 3 hours, or until the middle has cooked through. Cool in the pan. To release the cake from the sides of the pan, cut around the edge with a paring knife dipped in warm water. Run the knife around the sides several times, release the spring, and remove the cheesecake from the pan. Garnish the top with extra lime zest, orange zest, or candied lime slices. Slice and serve.

# TRES LECHES CRÈME BRÛLÉE

I order crème brûlée almost anywhere I go. It's my favorite way to finish a meal. This particular recipe is the richest version I've ever tasted. **Serves 8**

1¼ cups heavy cream
6 tablespoons sweetened
    condensed milk
6 tablespoons evaporated milk
½ cup brown sugar, divided
½ vanilla bean, scraped
Pinch of salt
4 egg yolks
2 tablespoons plus 2 teaspoons
    white sugar, divided
Berries, for garnish (blueberries,
    blackberries, strawberries—use
    2-3 of each berry type)

In a medium saucepan, heat cream, condensed milk, evaporated milk, ¼ cup brown sugar, and vanilla bean. Bring to a boil and then turn off the heat.

In a large mixing bowl, whisk together remaining brown sugar, salt, and egg yolks until smooth. While whisking vigorously, very gradually pour hot cream mixture into bowl with eggs and sugar; begin with just a few drops and then slowly increase the flow of hot cream until it's incorporated. It's very important to start slowly to keep the eggs from cooking at this point. Be sure to keep whisking while the cream mixture is being poured. Strain the mixture to ensure no lumps have formed. Pour into 8-ounce ramekins. Place the ramekins in a baking dish and then fill the dish with water halfway up the sides of the ramekins. Cover loosely with foil and bake in a 325-degrees F oven (not convection) for 45 to 60 minutes, or just until the mixture has set. Lightly jiggle one to see if the middle has set. Once set, refrigerate until cool. Just prior to serving, sprinkle a teaspoon of sugar over the top of each and spread evenly. Burn the sugar with a blowtorch until the sugar has melted and turned light brown. Top with a few fresh berries for garnish and serve.

# DUBLIN DR. PEPPER FLOAT WITH CINNAMON BUNUELO COOKIES

The original formula for Dr. Pepper is only available from the folks in Dublin, Texas. It's far superior to the regular brand, and true Texans travel from miles around just to stock up on the original. **Serves 1**

**Cookies**
2 flour tortillas
2 tablespoons sugar
½ tablespoon ground cinnamon
2 quarts canola oil

**Float**
1 bottle Dublin Original Dr. Pepper
2 scoops premium vanilla ice cream
2-3 tablespoons whipped cream

**Cinnamon Bunuelo Cookies**
Cut the tortillas into any shape desired. (At the restaurant, we make them into stars and the shape of Texas with cookie cutters; we also cut into thin strips for garnish.) Mix the sugar and cinnamon together. Fry the tortillas in 350-degree F vegetable oil until crispy. While the tortillas are still hot and fresh from the oil, sprinkle with cinnamon sugar until well coated.

**Dublin Dr. Pepper Float**
Freeze a glass prior to making the float. Place 2 scoops of ice cream into the frosted glass and then slowly pour in the Dr. Pepper. To serve, top with whipped cream and strips of Cinnamon Bunuelo Cookies.

# BONNELL'S CHOCOLATE CHIP COOKIE MARTINI

This particular martini makes the perfect end to a meal when dessert just seems to be more than you can handle. It's like getting dessert in a glass. **Serves 1**

---

1 tablespoon Navan (Natural Vanilla
    Liqueur from Grand Marnier)
1¹/₂ tablespoons amaretto
3 tablespoons chocolate vodka
¹/₄ cup Bailey's Irish Cream
2 teaspoons chocolate shavings,
    for garnish
Pinch of freshly grated nutmeg,
    for garnish

In a bar shaker, thoroughly shake all ingredients except chocolate and nutmeg with one scoop of ice. Strain and serve in a chilled martini glass.

Garnish with chocolate shavings and nutmeg.

---

# WHITE CHOCOLATE MARTINI

The slightly thick nature of the Godiva liqueur froths up well when shaken over ice, allowing the chocolate shavings to float on top of this creamy cocktail. **Serves 1**

---

¹/₄ cup Godiva White Chocolate
    Liqueur
2 tablespoons white crème de
    cocoa liqueur
3 tablespoons chocolate-flavored
    vodka (I prefer the Three Olives
    Brand)
2 teaspoons chocolate shavings,
    for garnish

Pour liquid ingredients into a bar shaker with one scoop of ice. Shake thoroughly. Strain and pour into a chilled martini glass; sprinkle with chocolate shavings.

---

# BONNELL'S BRANDY ICE

This is really somewhat of a milkshake all grown up. It's simple to make and irresistible. **Serves 3**

2 tablespoons plus 1½ teaspoons
  E&J brandy
1½ tablespoons Kahlúa
1½ tablespoons white Crème
  de Cacao
2 tablespoons Godiva White
  Chocolate Liqueur
2 tablespoons heavy cream
2 scoops vanilla ice cream
3 scoops cinnamon ice cream
Pinch of ground cinnamon
2 teaspoons chocolate shavings

Combine all liquid ingredients in a glass. Place the ice cream in a bar blender, add the liquid mixture; and blend until smooth. Pour into a brandy snifter and garnish with a dash of ground cinnamon and a sprinkle of chocolate shavings.

# MINT CHOCOLATE CHIP SMOOTHIE

Here's an easy cocktail to serve in place of dessert. These flavors of mint and chocolate are a real classic and quite a crowd pleaser. **Serves 1**

3 tablespoons heavy whipping cream
1 tablespoon Rumplemintz
2 tablespoons Godiva Dark
  Chocolate Liqueur
1 tablespoon plus 1½ teaspoons
  green crème de menthe
3–4 scoops vanilla ice cream
2 teaspoons chocolate shavings,
  for garnish

Combine all liquids in a glass. Place the ice cream in a bar blender, pour the liquids over the top, and blend until smooth. Pour into a brandy snifter and garnish with chocolate shavings.

BONNELL'S
Restaurant & Bar

# SMOKEHOUSE COCKTAIL

It's very difficult to explain how mesquite can make its way into a cocktail, but this western-style drink reminds me of the smells of leather from a saddle shop, combined with the sweet tobacco notes of a fine cigar shop. **Serves 1**

¼ cup McKendrick's Mesquite-
    Aged Western Whiskey
¼ cup sour mix
Splash of Coke
1 maraschino cherry, for garnish

Pour liquid ingredients over ice and garnish with a cherry or lemon slice.

# TEXAS SUNSET

Similar to a tequila sunrise, this drink is as pretty in the glass as it is on the palate. **Serves 1**

---

**¼ cup plus 1 tablespoon Bacardi Limon**
**2 tablespoons Cointreau**
**1 tablespoon cranberry juice**
**1 tablespoon gold tequila**
**1 tablespoon plus 1½ teaspoons Grenadine**
**Twist of lemon**

Mix all ingredients except for grenadine and lemon in a bar shaker with one scoop of ice and shake well to chill. Strain well and pour into a chilled martini glass. Pour the grenadine in last to make that perfect sunset look. Garnish with a twist of lemon or a maraschino cherry.

# ULTIMATE COWTOWN COSMO

The cosmopolitan has been resurrected over the last several years, but this version is my favorite that I have ever tasted. **Serves 1**

3 tablespoons Grey Goose L'Orange
   Vodka
1 tablespoon plus 1½ teaspoons
   Cointreau
¼ cup cranberry juice
Twist of lime

Add all ingredients except lime to a bar shaker with one scoop of ice. Shake well, strain, and pour into a chilled martini glass. Garnish with a twist of lime.

★ ★ ★

# INDEX

★ ★ ★

## METRIC CONVERSION CHART

### LIQUID AND DRY MEASURES

| U.S. | Canadian | Australian |
|---|---|---|
| ¼ teaspoon | 1 mL | 1 ml |
| ½ teaspoon | 2 mL | 2 ml |
| 1 teaspoon | 5 mL | 5 ml |
| 1 tablespoon | 15 mL | 20 ml |
| ¼ cup | 50 mL | 60 ml |
| ⅓ cup | 75 mL | 80 ml |
| ½ cup | 125 mL | 125 ml |
| ⅔ cup | 150 mL | 170 ml |
| ¾ cup | 175 mL | 190 ml |
| 1 cup | 250 mL | 250 ml |
| 1 quart | 1 liter | 1 litre |

### TEMPERATURE CONVERSION CHART

| Fahrenheit | Celsius |
|---|---|
| 250 | 120 |
| 275 | 140 |
| 300 | 150 |
| 325 | 160 |
| 350 | 180 |
| 375 | 190 |
| 400 | 200 |
| 425 | 220 |
| 450 | 230 |
| 475 | 240 |
| 500 | 260 |